HANDBOOK
—— to ——
$\mathcal{W}$ISDOM

Kenneth Boa, General Editor

Also by Kenneth D. Boa

Handbook to Scripture:
Integrating the Bible into Everyday Life

Face to Face Volume 1:
Praying the Scriptures for Intimate Worship

Face to Face Volume 2:
Praying the Scriptures for Spiritual Growth

Conformed to His Image: Biblical and Practical
Approaches to Spiritual Formation

Sense and Nonsense about Heaven and Hell

Sense and Nonsense about Angels and Demons

HANDBOOK
— to —
*W*ISDOM

Biblical Insights for Everyday Life

Kenneth Boa, General Editor

ZONDERVAN®

We want to hear from you. Please send your comments about this
book to us in care of zreview@zondervan.com. Thank you.

ZONDERVAN

Handbook to Wisdom
© 2007 by Kenneth Boa. All rights reserved.

Requests for information should be addressed to:

Zondervan, *Grand Rapids, Michigan 49530*

Library of Congress Control Number: 2011935171

Printed in the United States of America

11 12 13 14 15 16 17 18 /DCI/ 17 16 15 14 13 12 11 10 9 8 7 6 5 4 3 2

Dedication

This book is dedicated to my wife Karen,
our daughter Heather,
our son-in-law Matthew,
and our grandson Kenneth.

The Lord bless you and keep you;
The Lord make His face shine upon you
And be gracious to you;
The Lord turn His face toward you
And give you peace.

(Numbers 6:24-26)

 හ

Contents

Praise

"**To worship is**
to quicken the conscience
by the holiness of God,
to feed the mind
with the truth of God,
to purge the imagination
by the beauty of God,
to open up the heart
to the love of God,
to devote the will
to the purpose of God."

—*William Temple*

Introduction to Praise

There is no higher calling than to love and worship the infinite and personal God of creation and redemption. A. W. Tozer observed that what comes into our minds when we think about God is the most important thing about us.

Our image of God shapes our spiritual direction and future, and is forged in the times we spend in communion with Him. In complete contrast to the world, God's economy measures greatness not in terms of ability or accomplishments, but in the vitality and integrity of a person's walk with the Lord.

When we take time to meditate on the timeless truths of God's revealed Word, we expand our vision of the living God. In this way we develop a renewed perspective about the things that really matter in this world and in the world to come.

Day 1

Lord, I praise you because . . .

You are my strength and my song.

I will sing to the Lord, for He is highly exalted.
The Lord is my strength and my song;
He has become my salvation.
He is my God, and I will praise Him,
my father's God, and I will exalt Him.

(Exodus 15:1-2)

Lord God,

My heart is filled to overflowing with your praises, for I have seen Your mighty hand at work as You protect me from my enemies. You lift me up with Your outstretched arm and sit me securely in Your presence, high above problems and circumstances of my everyday life. You are my God, and the hope of my life. Therefore, I will praise and worship You with all my heart.

Amen.

Day 2

Lord, I praise you because . . .

Your lovingkindness endures forever.

I will give thanks to the Lord, for He is good;
His lovingkindness endures forever.
I will give thanks to the Lord for His unfailing love
and His wonderful acts to the children of men,
for He satisfies the thirsty soul
and fills the hungry soul with good things.

(Psalm 107:1, 8-9)

Dear Lord,

I gratefully acknowledge the blessings of Your faithfulness, goodness, and lovingkindness. Your perfect character never changes, and Your love never fails. You have satisfied my thirsty soul, and You have filled my hungry soul with good things. I thank You for Your wonderful acts on behalf of those who look to You.

Amen.

Day 3

Lord, I praise you because . . .

You are my great high priest.

Since I have a great high priest who has passed
through the heavens, Jesus the Son of God,
I will hold firmly to the faith I confess.
For I do not have a high priest who is unable to
sympathize with my weaknesses,
but one who has been tempted in every way,
just as I am, yet without sin.
Therefore, I will approach the throne of grace with
confidence, so that I may receive mercy and
find grace to help in time of need.

(Hebrews 4:14-16)

Lord Jesus,

You are my great high priest who came down from
heaven to seek and to save those who were lost.
Having completed Your work of redemption on earth,
You returned to the right hand of the Father where You
intercede for Your people as our high priest. Because You
know what it is to suffer and experience temptation, You
can sympathize with my weaknesses. I rejoice that I can
approach Your throne of grace with confidence that I will
receive Your mercy and grace in my times of need.

Amen.   8

Day 4

Lord, I praise you because . . .

Your power is greater than anything I can imagine.

God is able to do immeasurably more
than all that we ask or think,
according to His power that is at work within us.
To Him be glory in the church
and in Christ Jesus throughout all generations,
for ever and ever.

(Ephesians 3:20-21)

Lord,

I will give thanks for Your greatness, majesty, strength, and dominion. Your power is greater than anything I can imagine, and it is this boundless resurrection power that is at work in the lives of Your people. May I glorify, bless, and honor Your holy name with my lips and with my life.

Amen.

Day 5

Lord, I praise you because . . .

Your faithfulness is everlasting.

I will enter the Lord's gates with thanksgiving
and His courts with praise;
I will give thanks to Him and bless His name.
For the Lord is good and His lovingkindness
endures forever;
His faithfulness continues through all generations.

(Psalm 100:4-5)

Lord God,

I will give thanks to You and bless Your name, because
Your faithfulness is everlasting. When I pause and
remember Your many tender mercies, I am filled with
gratitude. May I delight in Your goodness and in Your
faithfulness, as I choose to revel in Your presence and
promises rather than dwell on the temporary problems
and setbacks of this life.

Amen.

&

Day 6

Lord, I praise you because . . .

You are great in counsel and mighty in deed.

Ah, Lord God!
You have made the heavens and the earth
by Your great power and outstretched arm.
Nothing is too difficult for You.
You are the great and mighty God,
whose name is the Lord of hosts.
You are great in counsel and mighty in deed,
and Your eyes are open to all the ways of the
sons of men;
You reward everyone according to his ways
and according to the fruit of his deeds.

(Jeremiah 32:17-19)

Lord God,

When I consider the marvels of the created order, the wonders of this world, and the awesome expanse of the heavens, I realize that nothing is too difficult for You. You are the Lord of hosts, and You know and rule all things. You are great in counsel and mighty in deed, and nothing is hidden from Your sight. Therefore I will praise You and magnify Your name.

Amen.

Day 7

Lord, I praise you because . . .

Your right hand is filled with righteousness.

Great is the Lord,
and most worthy of praise in the city of our God,
His holy mountain.
As is Your name, O God,
so is Your praise to the ends of the earth;
Your right hand is filled with righteousness.

(Psalm 48:1, 10)

O God,

You are indeed high and lifted up and Your greatness exceeds anything my limited mind can imagine. Surely You are most worthy of praise and exaltation and worship, because Your name is holy and awesome. Your right hand is filled with every perfection of goodness, righteousness, and truth.

Amen.

Day 8

Lord, I praise you because . . .

You are the blessed and only Sovereign.

God is the blessed and only Sovereign,
the King of kings and Lord of Lords,
who alone has immortality
and dwells in unapproachable light,
whom no one has seen or can see.
To Him be honor and eternal dominion.

(1 Timothy 6:15b-16)

Lord God,

You are blessed above all else, and Your sovereignty is complete and perfect. All things are under Your authority, and You alone traverse eternity past to eternity future. You dwell in such radiance that nothing in the created order can fully behold the splendor of Your boundless glory.

Amen.

Day 9

Lord, I praise you because . . .

You are eternally good.

I will give thanks to the Lord, for He is good;
His lovingkindness endures forever.

(Psalm 118:1)

Lord,

It is with a heart of gratitude and thanksgiving that
I approach You. All things come from You, and I
acknowledge my utter dependence on You for all that
I have and for my very life. You are the supreme good,
and Your lovingkindness and mercy on behalf of men and
angels are boundless and timeless.

Amen.

Day 10

Lord, I praise you because . . .

Your thoughts are greater than what I can imagine.

"My thoughts are not your thoughts,
neither are your ways My ways," declares the Lord.
"As the heavens are higher than the earth,
so are My ways higher than your ways,
and My thoughts than your thoughts."

(Isaiah 55:8-9)

O Lord,

My finite intellect cannot begin to mine the depths of Your Word and wisdom. Your revelation in the created order and in Scripture is full of wonder and mystery, and it is for me to acknowledge these limits when I am tempted to question Your ways. When I submit my mind to Your revealed Word, I discover things I could never have known or imagined.

Amen.

❧

Day 11

Lord, I praise you because . . .

*Your faithfulness continues through
all generations.*

Your word is settled in heaven forever, O Lord.
Your faithfulness continues through all generations;
You established the earth, and it stands.
They continue to this day according to Your ordinances,
for all things serve You.

(Psalm 119:89-91)

Lord,

You are the creator of the heavens and the earth, of all things visible and invisible. All creatures owe their existence to You, and Your wisdom is evident in the elegance and complexity of the earth and the creatures that inhabit it. Your faithfulness extends through all time, and all things serve You.

Amen.

∞

Day 12

Lord, I praise you because . . .

Your mercies never cease.

I call this to mind, and therefore I have hope:
The Lord's mercies never cease,
for His compassions never fail.
They are new every morning;
great is Your faithfulness.

(Lamentations 3:21-23)

Dear Lord,

In spite of the sorrows, disappointments, and setbacks in this life, I know that I can walk in hope because of Your ceaseless mercies. In Your eternal purposes, You redeem the things that appear hopeless in this world. Because Your mercies and compassions never fail, I will declare Your faithfulness and rejoice in hope.

Amen.

Day 13

Lord, I praise you because . . .

Your work is splendid and majestic.

Great are the works of the Lord;
they are pondered by all who delight in them.
Splendid and majestic is His work,
and His righteousness endures forever.
He has caused His wonderful acts to be remembered;
the Lord is gracious and compassionate.

(Psalm 111:2-4)

Lord God,

Your majestic works are evident to the wise and pondered by those who enjoy them and wonder at them. Your craftsmanship is splendid and exquisite, and Your righteousness prevails against all that would rise up against it. Your acts of grace and compassion are worthy of all praise and remembrance.

Amen.

Day 14

Lord, I praise you because . . .

You have done great things for me.

My soul magnifies the Lord
and my spirit rejoices in God my Savior,
for the Mighty One has done great things for me,
and holy is His name.
His mercy is on those who fear Him,
from generation to generation.

(Luke 1:46-47, 49-50)

Dear God,

My soul magnifies Your great and holy name, and my spirit rejoices in acknowledging Your salvation. You are the Mighty One who has accomplished so many great and glorious things in the lives of Your people, and Your holy name is to be extolled and feared in all generations of Your people.

Amen.

Day 15

Lord, I praise you because . . .

Your lovingkindness and faithfulness are ever-present.

It is good to give thanks to the Lord
and to sing praises to Your name, O Most High,
to declare Your lovingkindness in the morning
and Your faithfulness at night.

(Psalm 92:1-2)

O Most High,

Your glorious name is honored in heaven and on earth, and I join in the choruses of praise and thanksgiving as I reflect on Your lovingkindness each morning and on Your many acts of faithfulness and tender mercies through the day. You sustain me and give me hope and joy.

Amen.

— ∞ —

Day 16

Lord, I praise you because . . .

Your judgments are unsearchable.

Oh, the depth of the riches
both of the wisdom and knowledge of God!
How unsearchable are His judgments,
and His ways past finding out!
For who has known the mind of the Lord?
Or who has been His counselor?
Or who has first given to Him,
that He should repay him?
For from Him and through Him
and to Him are all things.
To Him be the glory forever! Amen.

(Romans 11:33-36)

Lord God,

Your wisdom and knowledge are unsearchable and beyond human comprehension. You require no counselor, and You have no needs. Instead, all things come from You and through You and to You, and You are exalted forever. The depth of Your boundless riches are past finding out.

Amen.

Day 17

Lord, I praise you because . . .

Your ways are righteous and true.

Great and marvelous are Your works,
Lord God Almighty!
Righteous and true are Your ways, King of the nations!
Who will not fear You, O Lord, and glorify Your name?
For You alone are holy.
All nations will come and worship before You,
for Your righteous acts have been revealed.

(Revelation 15:3-4)

Lord God Almighty,

I gratefully acknowledge that Your works are great and marvelous, and that Your ways are righteous and true. You are the sovereign Lord of all history and the true King of the nations. Your kingdom alone will prevail, and all knees will bow and acknowledge Your holy name and Your righteous acts.

Amen.

Day 18

Lord, I praise you because . . .

You are a righteous God and a Savior.

You, the Lord, alone have declared
what is to come from the distant past.
There is no God apart from You,
a righteous God and a Savior;
there is none besides You.
You are God, and there is no other.

(Isaiah 45:21-22)

Lord God,

You are the only Savior—holy, pure, altogether lovely, and glorious. There is none besides You, and no person or thing other than You is worthy of worship. In the distant past You revealed that which was to come, and Your promises are sure and steadfast.

Amen.

Day 19

Lord, I praise you because . . .

You are the Father of mercies.

Blessed be the God and Father of our Lord Jesus Christ,
the Father of mercies and the God of all comfort.

(2 Corinthians 1:3)

Father of our Lord Jesus Christ,

It gives me great encouragement to know that You are
the Father of mercies and the God of all comfort.
Because of Your good, loving, and unchanging character,
I can wholly trust in Your promises and in the timeless
truths of Your Word.

Amen.

ɛʊ

Day 20

Lord, I praise you because . . .

You are the everlasting God.

Lord, You have been our dwelling place
throughout all generations.
Before the mountains were born
or You brought forth the earth and the world,
from everlasting to everlasting, You are God.
You turn men back into dust,
and say, "Return, O children of men."
For a thousand years in Your sight
are like yesterday when it passes by or like a
watch in the night.

(Psalm 90:1-4)

Lord,

I marvel at the concept of your eternality—You are the
uncaused I AM THAT I AM whose nature is always to
exist. From everlasting to everlasting, You always are,
inhabiting Your temporal creation, but not limited to it.
By contrast, my years on this earth are but a tiny moment.
Yet You have given me the hope of everlasting life
through the life of Christ that is now indwells me.

Amen.

Day 21

Lord, I praise you because . . .

Your thoughts are precious to me.

How precious are Your thoughts to me, O God!
How vast is the sum of them!
If I should count them, they would outnumber the
grains of sand.
When I awake, I am still with You.

(Psalm 139:17-18)

O God,

Your thoughts are vast and all-encompassing,
surpassing all the grains of sand on all the beaches of
the world. You know all things and all people, and no one
can search out the wonders of Your thoughts. You never
leave me, even in my sleep; I am still with You when I
awake, and You are with me throughout the course of
each day.

Amen.

Day 22

Lord, I praise you because . . .

Your power and understanding are boundless.

"To whom will you compare Me?
Or who is My equal?" says the Holy One.
Lift your eyes to the heavens and see who has created them,
He who brings out the starry host by number
and calls them each by name.
Because of His great might and the strength of His power,
not one of them is missing.
Do you not know? Have you not heard?
The everlasting God, the Lord,
the Creator of the ends of the earth,
does not grow tired or weary.
No one can fathom His understanding.

(Isaiah 40:25-26, 28)

Everlasting God,

No one can compare with You, the infinite and personal creator of the heavens and the earth. You spoke the vast array of stars into being and know them each by name, though their number is stupendous. You order and control all things through Your sovereign power, and nothing escapes Your lordship. You rule all things in Your universe, and I can trust You to order my life as well.

Amen.

Day 23

Lord, I praise you because . . .

Your years will have no end.

My days are like a lengthened shadow,
and I wither away like grass.
But You, O Lord, will endure forever,
and the remembrance of Your name to all generations.
Of old, You laid the foundations of the earth,
and the heavens are the work of Your hands.
They will perish, but You will endure;
they will all wear out like a garment.
Like clothing, You will change them,
and they will be discarded.
But You are the same, and Your years will have no end.

(Psalm 102:11-12, 25-27)

O Lord,

Though all things in this created order are subject to change and decay, You never change, and Your power and years are never diminished. You who laid the foundations of the earth and spoke the heavens into being will also create new heavens and a new earth that will endure.

Amen.

Day 24

Lord, I praise you because . . .

Your years will have no end.

O Lord, You have searched me and You know me.
You know when I sit down and when I rise up;
You understand my thoughts from afar.
You scrutinize my path and my lying down
and are acquainted with all my ways.
Before a word is on my tongue,
O Lord, You know it completely.

(Psalm 139:1-4)

O Lord,

You know me down to the very depths of my inner
being. My ways and my paths are never hidden from
You, and You are fully aware of all my thoughts. I cannot
hide from You, but it gives me great comfort to realize that
the One who knows me best is also the One who loves me
most.

Amen.

Day 25

Lord, I praise you because . . .

Your judgments are true and righteous.

Hallelujah! Salvation and glory and power
belong to our God,
because His judgments are true and righteous.

(Revelation 19:1-2)

Lord God,

My hope is in Your unchanging character and in the
promises that flow out of Your goodness. I rejoice
that salvation and glory and power belong to You, for You
are the source of every good thing. Your judgments are
true and altogether righteous, and Your perfections are
lacking in nothing. I praise You for Your goodness.

Amen.

Day 26

Lord, I praise you because . . .

You rule over all the kingdoms of the nations.

O Lord, the God of our fathers,
are You not the God who is in heaven?
Are You not the ruler over all the kingdoms
of the nations?
Power and might are in Your hand,
and no one is able to withstand You.

(2 Chronicles 20:6)

God of all,

You are the ruler over all the kingdoms of the nations. You raise up and depose the kingdoms of this earth, but only Your kingdom is everlasting. Nothing can thwart Your good and perfect purposes, for You alone are the God of heaven. I delight in Your power, in Your sovereign rule, and in Your loving purposes for those whose hearts are fixed on You.

Amen.

Day 27

Lord, I praise you because . . .

You are the God of our salvation.

You answer us with awesome deeds of righteousness,
O God of our salvation,
You who are the hope of all the ends of the earth
and of the farthest seas;
You formed the mountains by Your strength,
having armed Yourself with power;
and You stilled the roaring of the seas,
the roaring of their waves, and the tumult of the peoples.

(Psalm 65:5-7)

God of my salvation,

I rejoice in Your awesome deeds of righteousness. The whole creation from the scale of the smallest to the greatest is filled with the evidences of Your magnificent beauty, glory, and boundless creativity. You have made all things well, and Your power is evident everywhere I look. May I walk in humility and gratitude before You, the God of my salvation.

Amen.

Day 28

Lord, I praise you because . . .

You are exalted on high.

From the rising of the sun to its setting,
the name of the Lord is to be praised.
The Lord is high above all nations,
His glory above the heavens.
Who is like the Lord our God,
the One who is enthroned on high,
who humbles Himself to behold
the things that are in the heavens and in the earth?

(Psalm 113:3-6)

Lord God,

You are the One who is enthroned on high, and Your glorious name is to be praised and exalted. Your majesty and splendor transcend all things, and yet You have humbled Yourself to behold and to be concerned with the things that are in the heavens and in the earth. In light of this, I marvel at the meaning of the incarnation of Your Son and at the suffering He bore to purchase our salvation.

Amen.

Day 29

Lord, I praise you because . . .

You rule over all Your creation.

The Lord God of hosts—
He who touches the earth and it melts,
and all who live in it mourn;
He who builds His staircase in the heavens
and founded the expanse over the earth;
He who calls for the waters of the sea
and pours them out over the face of the earth—
the Lord is His name.

(Amos 9:5-6)

Lord God of hosts,

The glories of the heavens and of the earth all point to You. Your authority and power are evident in the sea and in the sky, in the sun and moon and the starry hosts in the vast expanse of space. All these are in Your hands, and nothing can defeat Your purposes which You planned from before the foundation of the earth, even from all eternity.

Amen.

Day 30

Lord, I praise you because . . .

Your dominion endures through all generations.

All Your works will praise you, O Lord,
and Your saints will bless You.
They will speak of the glory of Your kingdom
and talk of Your power,
so that all men may know of Your mighty acts
and the glorious majesty of Your kingdom.
Your kingdom is an everlasting kingdom,
and Your dominion endures through all generations.

(Psalm 145:10-13)

O Lord,

Though the kingdoms and works of this earth all perish, Your kingdom and mighty works will endure forever. I rejoice in Your dominion that endures through all generations and in the glorious majesty of Your kingdom. May I speak of Your glory and of Your power, and may I magnify Your glorious name forever.

Amen.

ଏଓ

Day 31

Lord, I praise you because . . .

You give all men life and breath.

God, who made the world and everything in it,
since He is Lord of heaven and earth,
does not dwell in temples built by hands.
And He is not served by human hands,
as though He needed anything,
since He Himself gives all men life and breath
and everything else.

(Acts 17:24-25)

Lord God,

You are Lord of the entire cosmos. You made the world and everything in it, and You sustain Your creatures by giving them life and breath and providing for their needs. You have no needs, but You choose to want us and to love us. May I worship You in Spirit and in truth, glorifying Your holy name in the beauty of holiness.

Amen.

Day 32

Lord, I praise you because . . .

You created all things and sustain them.

Christ is the image of the invisible God,
the firstborn over all creation.
For by Him all things were created that are in heaven
and on earth,
visible and invisible,
whether thrones or dominions
or rulers or authorities;
all things were created by Him and for Him.
And He is before all things,
and in Him all things hold together.

(Colossians 1:15-17)

Lord Christ,

You created all things in heaven and on earth. All things
come from You and for You, and You are before all
things. Your dominion extends from the heavens to
the earth, and from the visible to the invisible. All angelic
beings are under Your divine authority, and Your
kingdom is everlasting.

Amen.

Day 33

Lord, I praise you because . . .

You are gracious and compassionate.

I will express the memory of Your abundant goodness
and joyfully sing of Your righteousness.
The Lord is gracious and compassionate,
slow to anger, and great in lovingkindness.
The Lord is good to all,
and His tender mercies are over all His works.

(Psalm 145:7-9)

Lord,

I praise You because You are gracious and compassionate.
Your patience and lovingkindness are wonderful, and
Your goodness extends to all who seek You. I thank You
for Your many tender mercies that are so evident in my
life. When I reflect upon them, I realize that they extend
to many things for which I have not been grateful. I will
rejoice in Your righteousness and lift up Your holy name.

Amen.

Day 34

Lord, I praise you because . . .

You created all things.

You are worthy, our Lord and God,
to receive glory and honor and power,
for You created all things,
and by Your will they were created and have their being.

(Revelation 4:11)

Lord and God,

It is my pleasure to exalt and lift up Your great and marvelous name, for You alone are worthy to receive glory and honor and power. All things derive their being from You, and You order and sustain the universe. I will rejoice in Your perfections and powers and delight in the boundless wealth of Your goodness and love.

Amen.

Day 35

Lord, I praise you because . . .

*You keep Your covenant and mercy with
Your people.*

O Lord, God of Israel, there is no God like You
in heaven above or on earth below;
You keep Your covenant and mercy
with Your servants who walk before You
with all their heart.

(1 Kings 8:23; 2 Chronicles 6:14)

O Lord,

You are beyond human comprehension, and yet You
delight to commune with Your people. You have
entered into a covenant relationship with those who know
You, and Your mercy and grace extend into every facet of
our lives. As Your loving servant, may I walk before You
with all my heart and honor Your perfect name.

Amen.

40

❧

Day 36

Lord, I praise you because . . .

You will judge the world in righteousness.

The Lord reigns forever;
He has established His throne for judgment.
He will judge the world in righteousness,
and He will govern the peoples with justice.
The Lord will also be a refuge for the oppressed,
a stronghold in times of trouble.
Those who know Your name will trust in You,
for You, Lord, have never forsaken those who seek You.

(Psalm 9:7-10)

Lord God,

You are my sure refuge and stronghold in times of trouble. I can fully trust in You and look to You when I am distressed and cast down. You are the fountainhead of righteousness, justice, mercy, goodness, and grace, and You will not forsake those who seek You. Because of Your wonderful character and ways, I will praise and exalt Your name forever.

Amen.

Day 37

Lord, I praise you because . . .

Your holiness is beautiful.

The Lord is great and greatly to be praised;
He is to be feared above all gods.
For all the gods of the nations are idols,
but the Lord made the heavens.
Splendor and majesty are before Him;
strength and joy are in His place.
I will ascribe to the Lord glory and strength.
I will ascribe to the Lord the glory due His name
and worship the Lord in the beauty of holiness.

(1 Chronicles 16:25-29)

Dear Lord,

The beauty of Your holiness is beyond all mortal
comprehension. It is evident in Your creation, and in
Your Word, and in the person and work of Your Son. I
praise Your greatness, Your splendor, Your majesty, Your
strength, Your joy, and Your glory. I will acknowledge
the glory due Your name and worship You in the beauty
of holiness.

Amen.

Day 38

Lord, I praise you because . . .

You rise to show compassion.

The Lord longs to be gracious and rises to
show compassion.
For the Lord is a God of justice;
blessed are all those who wait for Him!

(Isaiah 30:18)

Lord God,

You are the absolute and perfect and unchanging
source of goodness and justice. Your grace permeates
Your words and Your works and Your ways. I will wait
upon You, rest in You, trust in You, and commit my ways
to You. You richly bless all who call upon Your name in
humility and expectation and hope.

Amen.

Day 39

Lord, I praise you because ...

Your way is perfect and proven.

As for God, His way is perfect;
the word of the Lord is proven.
He is a shield for all who take refuge in Him.
For who is God besides the Lord?
And who is the Rock except our God?

(2 Samuel 22:31-32)

Lord God,

All throughout history, the truth of Your Word and Your promises has been proven to those who have trusted in them. You have been a shield for all who have taken refuge in You. You give hope and purpose and meaning in this passing world as You prepare us for a new realm that will never fade or pass away. You are my Rock and fortress and deliverer throughout the passing storms of life.

Amen.

Day 40

Lord, I praise you because . . .

You uphold all things by Your powerful word.

The Son is the radiance of God's glory
and the exact representation of His being,
upholding all things by His powerful word.
After He cleansed our sins,
He sat down at the right hand of the Majesty on high,
having become as much superior to angels
as the name He has inherited is more excellent
than theirs.

(Hebrews 1:3-4)

Lord Jesus,

You radiate God's glory as the exact representation of His being. To see You is to see the Father, and to hear Your words is to listen to the voice of the Father. You who uphold all things by the word of Your power came down from heaven to cleanse us of our sins. You are seated at the right hand of the Majesty on high, and You are worshiped with the Father and with the Holy Spirit.

Amen.

Day 41

Lord, I praise you because . . .

You humble and You exalt.

The Lord brings death and makes alive;
He brings down to the grave and raises up.
The Lord sends poverty and wealth;
He humbles and He exalts.
He raises the poor from the dust
and lifts the needy from the ash heap,
to seat them with princes
and make them inherit a throne of honor.
For the foundations of the earth are the Lord's,
and He has set the world upon them.

(1 Samuel 2:6-8)

Lord,

You established the foundations of the earth, and You have determined our appointed times and the boundaries of our habitations. Our lives are in Your hand, and it is in Your sovereign counsel to raise up or depose, to exalt or humble, to give wealth or poverty. You alone know what is best for Your people, and You alone have the power to bring it about.

Amen.

Day 42

Lord, I praise you because . . .

Your work is perfect and just.

God is the Rock;
His work is perfect, for all His ways are just.
A God of faithfulness and without injustice,
upright and just is He.

(Deuteronomy 32:4)

Lord God,

You are upright and just in Your complete and everlasting faithfulness. There is no injustice in You, and You are completely trustworthy. You alone are the Rock, the unchanging One who never breaks His promises. Your work is always perfect, and Your ways are beyond human comprehension.

Amen.

Day 43

Lord, I praise you because . . .

You are the high and lofty One.

You are the high and lofty One who inhabits eternity,
whose name is holy.
You live in a high and holy place
but also with him who is contrite and lowly in spirit,
to revive the spirit of the lowly
and to revive the heart of the contrite.

(Isaiah 57:15)

Father in the heavenlies,

You inhabit eternity, and Your years have no
beginning or end. You dwell in exalted majesty and in
unimaginable holiness. And yet You have chosen to be
close to those who are contrite and lowly in spirit and to
revive their hearts and spirits as they look to You, hope in
You, and wait upon You.

Amen.

&

Day 44

Lord, I praise you because . . .

You fulfill the desire of those who fear You.

The Lord is near to all who call upon Him,
to all who call upon Him in truth.
He fulfills the desire of those who fear Him;
He hears their cry and saves them.
The Lord preserves all who love Him,
but all the wicked He will destroy.

(Psalm 145:18-20)

Lord,

I give thanks that You are indeed near to all who call upon You in truth. You satisfy the desire of all who look to You and trust in You and who fear Your holy name. You are the Savior and preserver of all who love You. You hold and protect Your people and keep them from destruction. I will hope in You and rejoice in Your salvation.

Amen.

Day 45

Lord, I praise you because . . .

You are in authority over all of human affairs.

Blessed be the name of God for ever and ever,
for wisdom and power belong to Him.
He changes the times and the seasons;
He raises up kings and deposes them.
He gives wisdom to the wise
and knowledge to those who have understanding.
He reveals deep and hidden things;
He knows what is in the darkness,
and light dwells with Him.

(Daniel 2:20-22)

Lord God,

All might, power, rule, dominion, and authority is Yours, holy God. I lift up Your great and glorious name and walk in amazement at Your goodness and grace. You rule over the affairs of men and nations, and You are the source of wisdom, knowledge, and understanding. You dwell in inapproachable light, and nothing is hidden from Your omniscient view.

Amen.

ॐ

Day 46

Lord, I praise you because . . .

You have done wonderful things.

O Lord, You are my God;
I will exalt You and praise Your name,
for You have done wonderful things,
things planned long ago in perfect faithfulness.

(Isaiah 25:1)

O Lord,

Even before the foundation of the earth, You chose Your people and called them to dwell with You in the joy and glory of holiness. Your wonders are inexhaustible, and Your councils are inscrutable. Who can grasp the fullness of Your will and Your ways? I will exalt You and praise Your holy name.

Amen.

Day 47

Lord, I praise you because . . .

You delight to show mercy and forgiveness.

Who is a God like You, who pardons iniquity
and passes over the transgression of the remnant
of His inheritance?
You do not stay angry forever but delight to show mercy.
You will have compassion on Your people;
You will tread their iniquities underfoot
and hurl all their sins into the depths of the sea.

(Micah 7:18-19)

Lord God,

There is no one like You—glorious in might and
authority, You also dwell with the lowly and delight to
bestow mercy upon them. In Your great compassion, You
overcome our iniquities and completely remove our
transgressions. I rejoice in Your wonderful compassion,
because it is the source of my life and hope.

Amen.

Day 48

Lord, I praise you because . . .

You reveal Yourself to those You have chosen.

Jesus rejoiced in the Holy Spirit, and said,
"I praise You, Father, Lord of heaven and earth,
because You have hidden these things from the
wise and learned,
and revealed them to little children.
Yes, Father, for this was well-pleasing in Your sight.
All things have been delivered to Me by My Father.
No one knows the Son except the Father,
and no one knows the Father except the Son
and those to whom the Son chooses to reveal Him."

(Matthew 11:25-27; Luke 10:21-22)

Father,

I rejoice with Your Son and Your Holy Spirit in Your
perfect wisdom. For You chose to reveal Your truth to
those who approach You with the trust and humility of
little children. I could never hope to know You unless the
Son had chosen to reveal You to me. The Lord Jesus is my
life and hope, and I give You thanks and praise that He
came down from heaven.

Amen.

&

Day 49

Lord, I praise you because . . .

You gave Yourself for our sins.

Our Lord Jesus Christ gave Himself for our sins
to rescue us from the present evil age,
according to the will of our God and Father,
to whom be glory for ever and ever.

(Galatians 1:3-5)

Lord Jesus,

You are my light and my salvation, and I will always
hope and trust in You. For You gave Yourself for my
sins to rescue me from the present evil age and to grant me
the joy of Your presence in the ages to come. All glory is
Yours, both now and forever. You are the Alpha and the
Omega, the First and the Last, the Beginning and the End.

Amen.

Day 50

Lord, I praise you because . . .

You are great, and Your name is mighty in power.

There is none like You, O Lord;
You are great, and Your name is mighty in power.
Who should not revere You, O King of the nations?
It is Your rightful due.
For among all the wise men of the nations and in all
their kingdoms,
there is no one like You.

(Jeremiah 10:6-7)

King of the nations,

Your great and glorious name is to be lifted up and magnified in all times and places, because it is Your rightful due. The rulers and authorities of this earth come and go, and their kingdoms last but for a moment before they disappear. But You inhabit all ages and are Lord of all that is on the earth and in the heavens. There is no one like You.

Amen.

Day 51

Lord, I praise you because . . .

You have visited and redeemed Your people.

Blessed be the Lord, the God of Israel,
because He has visited us and has redeemed His people.
He has raised up a horn of salvation for us
in the house of His servant David (as He spoke
by the mouth of His holy prophets of long ago),
salvation from our enemies and from the hand of all
who hate us — to show mercy to our fathers and to
remember His holy covenant, the oath He swore to our
father Abraham, to rescue us from the hand of
our enemies, and to enable us to serve Him without fear
in holiness and righteousness before Him all our days.

(Luke 1:68-75)

Lord God,

It is my honor and joy to serve You without fear in
holiness and righteousness before You all my days. You
are the author of our salvation and the keeper of the
covenant promises You have made through Your servants
the prophets. You have redeemed Your people through
the blood of the new covenant that was shed for us.
Therefore I will bless and glorify Your great name forever.

Amen.

Day 52

Lord, I praise you because . . .

You empower those who have trusted in You.

God's power toward us who believe
is according to the working of His mighty strength,
which He exerted in Christ when He raised Him from
the dead and seated Him at His right hand in the
heavenly realms, far above all rule and authority, power
and dominion, and every title that can be given,
not only in the present age but also in the one to come.

(Ephesians 1:19-21)

Dear God,

You exerted Your mighty strength when You raised Christ Jesus from the dead and seated Him at Your right hand in the heavenly places. You exalted Him far above all rule and authority and above all earthly and heavenly powers to a glorious dominion that will never end. I praise You that it is this same power that is working in my life because of my identification with Jesus in His death, burial, resurrection, and ascension.

Amen.

Day 53

Lord, I praise you because . . .

You are the first and the last.

The Lord Jesus is the first and the last,
and the Living One;
He was dead, and behold He is alive forevermore
and holds the keys of death and of Hades.

(Revelation 1:17-18)

Lord Jesus,

You are the first and the last, the Living One who has defeated death and holds the keys of death and of life. Your death brought about the death of death, and Your resurrection is the basis for our resurrection life. You have redeemed Your people — body, soul, and spirit — and they will be coheirs with You in the heavenly places in the ages to come.

Amen.

Day 54

Lord, I praise you because . . .

*You have shown Your greatness and
Your mighty deeds.*

O Lord God, You have shown Your servants
Your greatness and Your strong hand,
for what god is there in heaven or on earth
who can do the works and mighty deeds You do?

(Deuteronomy 3:24)

O Lord God,

You are utterly unique, magnificent, incomprehensible,
transcendent, majestic, holy, glorious, righteous,
perfect, and powerful. You dwell in the beauty of holiness
and in the splendor of majesty, and nothing in all creation
is like You, for You alone created all things for Your glory
and good pleasure.

Amen.

෨

Day 55

Lord, I praise you because . . .

You purchased us with Your blood.

You are worthy to take the scroll and to open its seals,
because You were slain,
and with Your blood You purchased men for God
from every tribe and language and people and nation.
You have made them to be a kingdom and priests
to serve our God, and they will reign on the earth.

(Revelation 5:9-10)

Lord Jesus,

I exalt You and praise Your holy name for purchasing
men for God from every tribe and language and people
and nation with Your blood. It was Your good pleasure to
call them to be a kingdom and priests to serve the living
God. You are worthy of all honor and praise, and it
is my joy and delight to call to mind Your perfections
and goodness.

Amen.

ॐ

Day 56

Lord, I praise you because ...

Your kingdom will endure forever.

Jesus will be great and will be called
the Son of the Most High.
The Lord God will give Him the throne of His father
David, and He will reign over the house of Jacob forever,
and His kingdom will never end.

(Luke 1:32-33)

Lord Jesus,

You are the Messiah, the anointed One, the fulfillment of the promises made in the law, the prophets, and the writings. All Scripture speaks of You and points to Your work as prophet, priest, and king. You will inherit the throne of David and reign over the earth in righteousness, justice, and truth.

Amen.

Day 57

Lord, I praise you because . . .

You gave Yourself to redeem us from all iniquity.

We are looking for the blessed hope and the glorious
appearing of our great God and Savior, Christ Jesus,
who gave Himself for us to redeem us from all iniquity
and to purify for Himself a people for His own
possession, zealous for good works.

(Titus 2:13-14)

Lord Jesus,

You are our great God and Savior, and I wait with
expectant and blessed hope for Your glorious
appearing. In Your love and obedience to the will of the
Father, You gave Yourself for us to redeem us from all
iniquity. I praise You that You have called me to be part of
a people for Your own possession, zealous for good
works.

Amen.

Day 58

Lord, I praise you because . . .

*You are worthy of all honor and glory
and blessing.*

John looked and heard the voice of many angels
encircling the throne and the living creatures and the
elders; and their number was myriads of myriads,
and thousands of thousands, saying with a loud voice,
"Worthy is the Lamb, who was slain,
to receive power and riches and wisdom
and strength and honor and glory and blessing!"

(Revelation 5:11-12)

Lord Jesus,

You are the Passover Lamb of God who takes away the
sins of the world. You humbled Yourself to the point
of death on the cross, and You have been exalted to receive
power and riches and wisdom and strength and honor
and glory and blessing. The whole host of heaven
praises You, and it is my delight to join the praises of this
glorious throng.

Amen.

Day 59

Lord, I praise you because . . .

Your name will be great among the nations.

From the rising to the setting of the sun,
Your name will be great among the nations.
In every place incense and pure offerings will be brought
to Your name, for Your name will be great
among the nations.

(Malachi 1:11)

Lord God,

Your name is great and wondrous, and it is to be
exalted among the nations. The day will come when
You return and Your will is done on earth as it is in
heaven. All nations will honor the Lord Jesus, and He will
reign on the throne of David. I worship You—Father, Son,
and Holy Spirit—and rejoice in Your glory and Your
salvation.

Amen.

೮

Day 60

Lord, I praise you because . . .

You have bestowed Your grace upon us.

God chose me in Christ before the foundation of the
world
to be holy and blameless in His sight.
In love He predestined me to be adopted as His son
through Jesus Christ,
according to the good pleasure of His will,
to the praise of the glory of His grace,
which He bestowed upon me in the One He loves.

(Ephesians 1:4-6)

Father,

I give thanks that in Your great love You chose me even
before the foundation of the world to be Your adopted
child through Your Son Jesus Christ. This was according
to the good pleasure of Your will and to the praise of the
glory of Your grace which You bestowed upon me in
Him. I rejoice that I have been embraced by Your love.

Amen.

Day 61

Lord, I praise you because . . .

You are compassionate and gracious.

The Lord, the Lord God,
is compassionate and gracious, slow to anger,
and abounding in lovingkindness and truth,
maintaining love to thousands,
and forgiving iniquity, transgression, and sin.

(Exodus 34:6-7)

Lord God,

I stand amazed at the beauty of Your attributes: Your perfect compassion, Your boundless grace, Your infinite patience, Your abundant lovingkindness, Your wonderful truth, Your intense love, and Your wonderful forgiveness. Because of who You are, I can walk in faith, hope, and love.

Amen.

—————————— ⍑ ——————————

Day 62

Lord, I praise you because . . .

You are the King eternal, immortal, invisible.

To the King eternal, immortal, invisible,
the only God,
be honor and glory forever and ever.

(1 Timothy 1:17)

O Lord my King,

In Your essence You are incomprehensible and mysterious. You have revealed that You are eternal, immortal, and invisible, and that Your transcendent majesty is boundless. And yet You choose to want us for Yourself and give us the gift of Your indwelling Spirit. To You be honor and glory forever and ever.

Amen.

Day 63

Lord, I praise you because . . .

You are mighty and awesome.

The Lord my God is God of gods
and Lord of lords, the great God,
mighty and awesome,
who shows no partiality and accepts no bribes.
He executes justice for the fatherless and the widow
and loves the alien, giving him food and clothing.

(Deuteronomy 10:17-18)

O Lord my God,

You are the mighty and awesome God of gods
and Lord of lords. I praise You that You show no
partiality and accept no bribes, but that You execute justice
for those who are in need. My hope is fixed on Your
unchanging character and on Your gracious promises,
and I give thanks for who You are.

Amen.

Day 64

Lord, I praise you because . . .

You are the author of our salvation.

A great multitude, which no one could number,
from all nations and tribes and peoples and languages
will stand before the throne and before the Lamb,
clothed with white robes with palm branches in their
hands, and will cry out with a loud voice,
"Salvation belongs to our God, who sits on the throne,
and to the Lamb!"

(Revelation 7:9-10)

Lord God,

Salvation belongs to the triune God—Father, Son, and
Holy Spirit. You chose us for Yourself, redeemed us
with the blood of Christ, and regenerated us through the
power of Your Holy Spirit. You are to be exalted and
magnified by the great host of Your creatures because of
who You are and what You have done.

Amen.

Day 65

Lord, I praise you because . . .

Your righteousness and wonders are measureless.

My mouth will tell of Your righteousness
and of Your salvation all day long,
though I know not its measure.
I will come in the strength of the Lord God;
I will proclaim Your righteousness, Yours alone.
Since my youth, O God, You have taught me,
and to this day I declare Your wondrous deeds.

(Psalm 71:15-17)

O God,

I will rejoice and exult in Your righteousness, a righteousness that is perfect, holy, pure, good, loving, patient, just, compassionate, and altogether lovely. It is through Your salvation that I have meaning and hope in this world, and Your presence is ever with me. It is Your strength that sustains me, and I will proclaim Your measureless righteousness and salvation to the glory of Your name.

Amen.

Day 66

Lord, I praise you because . . .

You love me and protect me.

Who shall separate me from the love of Christ?
Shall tribulation, or distress, or persecution,
or famine, or nakedness, or danger, or sword?
As it is written: "For Your sake we face death all day
long; we are considered as sheep to be slaughtered."
Yet in all these things I am are more than a conqueror
through Him who loved me.

(Romans 8:35-37)

Lord Jesus,

Nothing at all can separate me from Your causeless,
measureless, and ceaseless love. No person or force
in heaven, on earth, or under the earth can remove me
from Your loving grip, for You are Lord of all. In spite of
the afflictions, adversities, setbacks, and uncertainties of
this earthly life, I am secure in You.

Amen.

71

Day 67

Lord, I praise you because . . .

*You are worthy of glory, majesty, dominion,
and authority.*

To the only God our Savior,
through Jesus Christ our Lord,
be glory, majesty, dominion, and authority,
before all ages and now and forever. Amen.

(Jude 25)

Lord God,

You are the only God and Savior, and Jesus Christ is the glorious King of kings and Lord of lords who purchased us and liberated us from our bondage to sin and death. All glory, majesty, dominion, and authority is Yours, O Lord, before all ages, now, and forever.

Amen.

Day 68

Lord, I praise you because . . .

Your dominion is an eternal dominion.

The Most High is sovereign over the kingdoms of men
and gives them to whomever He wishes and sets over
them the lowliest of men. I will bless the Most High
and praise and honor Him who lives forever.
His dominion is an eternal dominion, and His kingdom
endures from generation to generation.
He regards all the inhabitants of the earth as nothing,
and does as He pleases with the host of heaven
and the inhabitants of the earth.
No one can hold back His hand or say to Him:
"What have You done?" I praise, exalt, and honor the
King of heaven, for all His works are true, and all
His ways are just, and He is able to humble those
who walk in pride.

(Daniel 4:17, 34-35, 37)

God Most High,

I will bless and honor You, the Most High, who lives
forever. You rule in the splendor of sovereignty over all
kingdoms and all creation, and Your dominion is
everlasting. You do all that You please with the host of
heaven and the inhabitants of the earth, and all Your
works are true and Your ways just. Your name is praised
above all.

Amen.   73

Day 69

Lord, I praise you because . . .

You are exalted as head over all.

Yours, O Lord, is the greatness and the power
and the glory and the victory and the majesty,
for everything in heaven and earth is Yours.
Yours, O Lord, is the kingdom, and You are exalted as
head over all. Both riches and honor come from You,
and You are the ruler of all things. In Your hand is
power and might to exalt and to give strength to all.
Therefore, my God, I give You thanks and praise Your
glorious name. All things come from You,
and I can only give You what comes from Your hand.

(1 Chronicles 29:11-14)

O Lord,

You are exalted as head over all things, and it is from
Your hand that every good gift is given. You are
awesome in power and in might, and all greatness, glory,
victory, and majesty is Yours, O Lord. I give You thanks
and bless and praise Your glorious name. All that I am
and have comes from You, and I offer myself to You as a
living sacrifice.

Amen.

Day 70

Lord, I praise you because . . .

You will treasure Your servants forever.

There will no longer be any curse.
The throne of God and of the Lamb will be in the new
Jerusalem, and His servants will serve Him.
They will see His face, and His name will be on their
foreheads. And there will be no night there;
they will not need the light of a lamp or the light of the
sun, for the Lord God will give them light.
And they shall reign for ever and ever.

(Revelation 22:3-5)

Lord God,

I look with great anticipation at the promise of Your
heavenly kingdom in which there will be no night, no
curse, no death, no sickness, no mourning, and no crying.
You will make all things new, and we will behold the light
and beauty of Your face. I praise You for the hope of
heaven and the glories of the age to come.

Amen.

Day 71

Lord, I praise you because ...

You have clothed me with the garments of salvation.

I will greatly rejoice in the Lord;
my soul will be joyful in my God.
For He has clothed me with garments of salvation
and arrayed me in a robe of righteousness,
as a bridegroom decks himself with ornaments,
and as a bride adorns herself with her jewels.

(Isaiah 61:10)

Lord God,

I bless and exalt Your high, majestic, wonderful, awesome, and holy name. My soul will rejoice in the Lord who has clothed me with the garments of salvation. You have arrayed me in the robe of the righteousness of Christ, and You have blessed me with His indwelling life. I praise You that You will come again and receive me to Yourself, so that were You are, there I will be also.

Amen.

Promises

Introduction to Promises

When we contemplate the gracefulness of a flower or the grandeur of a tree, we properly respond with aesthetic admiration. Similarly, we respond to our pets with personal affection, and at times to other people with self-giving love. If nature is worthy of admiration, animals of affection, and human beings of sacrificial love, how then should we respond to the infinite and personal Author of all biological and spiritual life? The biblical answer is clear—God alone is worthy of worship. Blessing and honor and glory and dominion forever belong to the Creator and Redeemer (Revelation 5:13), and every tongue in heaven, on earth, and under the earth, including all who have rebelled against Him, will confess this to be so (Philippians 2:10-11).

Let us rejoice as we prayerfully reflect on the wonderful promises in Scripture about God's principles, presence, provision, protection, plan, and preparation.

Day 72

*God is preparing a place for me
so that I can live with Him forever.*

In My Father's house are many dwellings;
if it were not so, I would have told you.
I am going there to prepare a place for you.
And if I go and prepare a place for you,
I will come again and receive you to Myself,
that you also may be where I am.

(John 14:2-3)

Lord Jesus,

Your love and care for me is beyond my imagination.
I can barely comprehend that You have prepared a
special place for me in Your Father's house. As I pause
throughout the day, I will dream of the warmth and
beauty of my heavenly home and with joy and
excitement, I will anticipate the day when I shall meet You
there and speak with You face to face.

Amen.

Day 73

God is in control of all things,
and He has my best interests at heart.

The Lord reigns; He is clothed with majesty;
the Lord is robed in majesty and is armed with strength.
Indeed, the world is firmly established;
it cannot be moved.
Your throne is established from of old;
You are from everlasting.
Your testimonies stand firm;
holiness adorns Your house, O Lord, forever.

(Psalm 93:1-2, 5)

O Lord,

It gives me real comfort to know that Your character never changes and that Your promises stand firm forever. Nothing can thwart Your good plans, and knowing this gives me great assurance in this world of turmoil, change, and uncertainty. My confidence is in Your goodness and majesty.

Amen.

Day 74

*Whatever I do for the sake of Jesus
will not be in vain, but will always endure.*

Thanks be to God,
who gives us the victory through our Lord Jesus Christ.
Therefore I will be steadfast, immovable,
abounding in the work of the Lord,
knowing that my labor in the Lord is not in vain.

(1 Corinthians 15:57-58)

Lord,

I am grateful for the victory that You have won for me through my Lord Jesus Christ. Because my life is now in Him, the things I do for His sake will go on into eternity. My labor is not in vain, but will bear lasting fruit as I walk in the power of Your Spirit.

Amen.

Day 75

Because I am now alive to Christ,
I am no longer under the dominion of sin.

If I died with Christ,
I believe that I will also live with Him,
knowing that Christ, having been raised from the dead,
cannot die again; death no longer has dominion over
Him. For the death that He died, He died to sin once for
all; but the life that He lives, He lives to God.
In the same way, I must consider myself to be dead to
sin, but alive to God in Christ Jesus.

(Romans 6:8-11)

Lord Jesus,

It is a marvel that I have died with You and that I will also
live with You in the ages to come. May I experience a
growing realization that since I am now alive to God in
Christ Jesus, I have died to the dominion of sin in my life.

Amen.

Day 76

*The Lord satisfies my spiritual thirst by
inviting me to drink freely from the water of life.*

You are the Alpha and the Omega,
the Beginning and the End.
To him who is thirsty,
You will give to drink without cost
from the spring of the water of life.
He who overcomes will inherit all this,
and You will be his God and he will be Your son.

(Revelation 21:6-7)

O Lord,

I rejoice that You are the Alpha and the Omega, the Beginning and the End, and I thank Your for Your invitation to drink without cost from the spring of the water of life. May I live in Your strength and lay hold of Your abundant inheritance.

Amen.

Day 77

*The Lord is my helper and keeper who
watches over my steps and preserves my soul.*

I lift up my eyes to the hills—where does
my help come from?
My help comes from the Lord, who made
heaven and earth.
He will not allow my foot to slip;
He who watches over me will not slumber.
The Lord is my keeper; the Lord is my shade
at my right hand.
The sun will not harm me by day, nor
the moon by night.
The Lord will keep me from all evil; He will
preserve my soul.
The Lord will watch over my coming and going
from this time forth and forever.

(Psalm 121:1-3, 5-8)

Lord,

I look to You for my help and protection in this uncertain
world. You protect me from evil and preserve my soul.
When I suffer pain and loss, even then I know that You
will use it for my ultimate good by drawing me ever
closer to You. My hope is centered on You and on Your
ever-present care.

Amen.

Day 78

Because I have trusted in Jesus,
I am assured of His resurrected life.

Jesus said to Martha, "I am the resurrection and the life. He who believes in Me will live, even though he dies, and whoever lives and believes in Me will never die."

(John 11:25-26)

Lord Jesus,

I give thanks for Your assurance that I have been delivered from the kingdom of sin and death and have been transferred to the kingdom of Your righteousness and life. Grant me the grace of growing trust in Your person and promises.

Amen.

Day 79

When I come closer to Christ,
He takes my burdens and gives me His peace.

Lord, You have said, "Come to Me,
all you who labor and are heavy laden, and
I will give you rest.
Take My yoke upon you and learn from Me,
for I am gentle and humble in heart,
and you will find rest for your souls.
For My yoke is easy, and My burden is light."

(Matthew 11:28-30)

Lord,

It is only in You that I can find rest for my soul. When I take Your yoke upon me and learn from You, I discover the ease of Your yoke and the lightness of Your burden. Grant me a growing awareness of Your peace and presence.

Amen.

Day 80

As I turn from dependence on myself
to dependence on Christ,
I discover His power in my life.

Your grace is sufficient for me,
for Your power is made perfect in weakness.
Therefore, I will boast all the more gladly
in my weaknesses,
that the power of Christ may rest upon me.
Therefore, I can be content in weaknesses,
in insults, in hardships, in persecutions,
in difficulties, for Christ's sake.
For when I am weak, then I am strong.

(2 Corinthians 12:9-10)

Lord God,

Teach me to realize that Your grace is always sufficient for me. It is foolish to rely on the weakness of the flesh when I can walk in the power of Christ who lives in me. May I discover His strength by acknowledging my weakness, even in those areas in which I am tempted to think I am competent.

Amen.

Day 81

*Those who serve and follow the Lord
will be honored by His presence.*

If anyone serves You, he must follow You;
and where You are, Your servant also will be.
If anyone serves You, the Father will honor him.

(John 12:26)

Lord Jesus,

May I learn to serve You and follow You wherever You lead me to go so that I will abide in You and enjoy Your manifest presence in my life. I am grateful that You honor those who serve You. Teach me what it means to serve You in the daily details of life.

Amen.

— ☙ —

Day 82

The sovereign Lord of creation rules
over all things,
and nothing can thwart His excellent purposes.

The Lord of hosts has sworn,
"Surely, as I have thought, so it will be,
and as I have purposed, so it will stand.
For the Lord of hosts has purposed, and
who can annul it?
His hand is stretched out, and who can turn it back?

(Isaiah 14:24, 27)

O Lord,

I revel in the goodness of Your intentions and plans, knowing that You always desire what is best for Your people. You rule over all that is in heaven and on earth and under the earth, and no purpose of Yours can be annulled. When You stretch out Your hand, nothing can turn it back.

Amen.

Day 83

*There is no comparison between
the afflictions of our brief earthly sojourn
and the glory of our eternal heavenly existence.*

I do not lose heart; even though my outward
man is perishing,
yet my inner man is being renewed day by day.
For this light affliction which is momentary
is working for me a far more exceeding and eternal
weight of glory,
while I do not look at the things which are seen
but at the things which are unseen.
For the things which are seen are temporary,
but the things which are unseen are eternal.

(2 Corinthians 4:16-18)

Heavenly Father,

The pains and uncertainties of my earthly life
sometimes tempt me to lose heart. But when I reflect
on the contrast between this momentary light adversity
and the endless weight of glory, intimacy, beauty, and
adventure in the heavenly realms in Your presence, I am
strengthened and encouraged.

Amen.

———————— &co; ————————

Day 84

*God Himself will perfect, confirm, strengthen,
and establish me in His heavenly kingdom.*

The God of all grace,
who called me to His eternal glory in Christ,
after I have suffered a little while,
will Himself perfect, confirm, strengthen,
and establish me.

(1 Peter 5:10)

God of all grace,

You transmute my very brief suffering on this earth into
eternal glory through Your boundless grace and
goodness. I will rest in the living hope of the inheritance
that You are preparing for those who Love You and have
come to know You through Your glorious Son.

Amen.

Day 85

*Jesus is the doorway for the
sheep of God's pasture,
and it is His good pleasure that those who are
called by Him will enjoy His abundant life.*

You are the door; whoever enters through You
will be saved and will come in and go out
and find pasture.
The thief comes only to steal and kill and destroy;
You have come that we may have life and
have it abundantly.

(John 10:9-10)

Lord Jesus,

It encourages and comforts me to know that You are the
Good Shepherd of my soul and that I can enjoy the
abundant pastures into which You guide me. You protect
me from my adversaries and deliver me from the snares
of death and destruction. You lead me in the way of
everlasting life.

Amen.

Day 86

*The Lord will reward all who have
longed for His appearing with
the crown of righteousness.*

I will fight the good fight, finish the race,
and keep the faith,
so that there will be laid up for me the
crown of righteousness,
which the Lord, the righteous Judge, will award
to me on that day;
and not only to me, but also to all who have
longed for His appearing.

(2 Timothy 4:7-8)

Lord,

I know that I am called to fight the good fight and to
finish the race You have set before me. May I be
faithful and obedient to Your heavenly calling, and may I
long more and more for your glorious appearing as I
anticipate seeing You face to face.

Amen.

Day 87

*Because I have been purchased by the blood
of Christ Himself, I know that God is
always for me.*

If God is for me, who can be against me?
He who did not spare His own Son,
but delivered Him up for us all,
how will He not, also with Him, freely give us all things?

(Romans 8:31-32)

Father,

In Your love and mercy, You sent forth Your Son so that
we would have life in His name. I thank You that
nothing can prevail against me and that You will freely
give me all things in Christ. May I live and walk in this
great truth today.

Amen.

&

Day 88

*Those who hunger and thirst for righteousness
will find satisfaction in Jesus.*

Blessed are those who hunger and thirst
for righteousness,
for they shall be satisfied.

(Matthew 5:6)

Lord Jesus,

This world with its constant appeals to vanity, comparison, and earthly wealth is too much with me. Give me the grace to hunger and thirst for the things You declare to be important. May I long for Your righteousness and realize that I possess all things in Christ.

Amen.

Day 89

God is the source of all pleasure and joy,
and He offers these to all who seek Him.

I have set the Lord always before me;
because He is at my right hand, I will not be shaken.
Therefore my heart is glad, and my glory rejoices;
my body also will rest in hope.
You will make known to me the path of life;
in Your presence is fullness of joy;
in Your right hand are pleasures forever.

(Psalm 16:8-9, 11)

Dear Lord,

You are indeed at my right hand, and it is from Your right hand that I receive the boundless abundance of Your joy and fullness. I will rest in hope and rejoice in the glory that You have set before me. Keep me on the path of life so that I will dwell in Your presence forever.

Amen.

Day 90

***God is always good to those
who seek Him and hope in Him.***

"The Lord is my portion," says my soul,
"therefore I will wait for Him."
The Lord is good to those who wait for Him,
to the soul who seeks Him.
It is good to hope silently for the salvation of the Lord.

(Lamentations 3:24-26)

Lord,

I will wait for You, seek You, rest in You, hope in You,
trust in You, and abide in You as I anticipate the fullness
of Your salvation. You have given me a real and living
hope during my sojourn in this life, and I know that You
will be my portion forever.

Amen.

Day 91

When I listen to the wisdom
from above, I will walk securely.

The waywardness of the simple will kill them,
and the complacency of fools will destroy them;
but whoever listens to wisdom will live securely
and be at ease from the fear of evil.

(Proverbs 1:32-33)

O Lord,

Keep me from being wayward and complacent. Guard
my paths and give me a growing desire to listen
carefully to Your wisdom and to walk in obedience to it.
When I seek You first, I will live securely and be at ease
from the fear of evil.

Amen.

Day 92

*God uses our afflictions to create
a life message that will serve others.*

God comforts us in all our afflictions,
so that we can comfort those in any affliction
with the comfort we ourselves have received from God.

(2 Corinthians 1:4)

O God,

You have shown me Your tender and severe mercies to train and discipline me in the way of trust, righteousness, and hope so that I will be empowered to minister to others out of my weakness and dependence upon You. May I welcome Your comfort so that I will in turn be able to comfort others.

Amen.

Day 93

God works in us both to will
and to act according to His good purpose.

I will work out my salvation with fear and trembling,
for it is God who works in me
to will and to act according to His good purpose.

(Philippians 2:12-13)

Lord,

May I work out that which You have worked into me.
Let me order my steps with fear and trembling,
knowing that apart from You, I can do nothing. Thank
You for the good purpose to which You have called me
and will call me. I want to live out this good purpose in
my desires and practices.

Amen.

⁎

Day 94

From eternity to eternity,
I am in the great grip of the living God.

Those God foreknew,
He also predestined to be conformed to the
likeness of His Son,
that He might be the firstborn among many brothers.
And those He predestined, He also called;
those He called, He also justified;
those He justified, He also glorified.

(Romans 8:29-30)

Dear Lord,

You have foreknown me, chosen me, called me, and justified me, and You will glorify me in Christ Jesus. Your purpose is nothing less than that I be fully conformed to the image of Your Son. May I live in hope of this great and glorious destiny.

Amen.

Day 95

The Word of the Lord lives and abides forever.

Heaven and earth will pass away,
but the words of the Lord Jesus will never pass away.

(Matthew 24:35; Luke 21:33)

Lord Jesus,

I thank You that in this world of change, loss, and uncertainty, there is something to which I can hold that will never disappoint me or disappear. I want Your Word to abide in me so that I will lay hold of that which is life indeed. Your Word is true and living and lasting.

Amen.

ℰ

Day 96

All who trust in Jesus have life in His name.

I believe that Jesus is the Christ,
the Son of God,
and by believing, I have life in His name.

(John 20:31)

Lord,

Thank You for the grace You have shown me by drawing me to Jesus and enabling me to trust in Him for the hope of eternal life. I have transferred my trust from the futility of my own works to the perfection of His life in me. He is the Anointed One who came to take away the sin of the world.

Amen.

Day 97

*All good gifts come from God
who has called us to be the children
of the new creation.*

Every good and perfect gift is from above,
coming down from the Father of lights,
with whom there is no variation, or shifting shadow.
Of His own will He brought us forth by
the word of truth,
that we might be a kind of firstfruits of His creatures.

(James 1:17-18)

Father of lights,

There is no variation or shifting shadow with You. Your purposes and gifts are always for my good, and You have brought me forth through Your living word of truth to become a new creation in Christ Jesus. May I walk in newness of life by faith in Him.

Amen.

∽

Day 98

*God has sealed and will protect all
who have trusted in Christ through
His Holy Spirit.*

I trusted in Christ when I heard the word of truth,
the gospel of my salvation.
Having believed, I was sealed in Him with
the Holy Spirit of promise,
who is a deposit guaranteeing my inheritance
until the redemption of those who are God's possession,
to the praise of His glory.

(Ephesians 1:13-14)

Lord,

By Your grace, I responded to the gospel of truth by
trusting in Christ for my salvation. You sealed me in
Him with Your Holy Spirit of promise and have assured
me of Your protection and preservation until I receive the
fullness of my inheritance in the heavenly realms.

Amen.

Day 99

*God is preparing a new heaven
and a new earth for those who are His own.*

There will be a new heaven and a new earth,
for the first heaven and the first earth will pass away,
and there will no longer be any sea.

(Revelation 21:1)

Lord God,

You have revealed that this present earth and its works will be burned up, and that You will create new heavens and a new earth that will never pass away. May I order my path in light of this coming new creation so that I will live in holy conduct and godliness.

Amen.

Day 100

Because I have trusted in Jesus,
I have eternal life and will not be condemned.

Whoever hears the word of Jesus and believes
Him who sent Him
has eternal life and will not come into judgment,
but has passed over from death to life.

(John 5:24)

Lord Jesus,

I have heard Your life-giving word and entrust myself
wholly to You. Thank You for the gift of Your eternal
life that dwells in me and for the realization that I will not
face a judgment of condemnation, since my sins have
been forgiven and I am a child of the new creation.

Amen.

Day 101

*Whenever God disciplines me, it is for
my ultimate good.*

Our fathers disciplined us for a little while
as they thought best,
but God disciplines us for our good, that we
may share in His holiness.
No discipline seems pleasant at the time, but painful;
later on, however, it produces the peaceable
fruit of righteousness
for those who have been trained by it.

(Hebrews 12:10-11)

Lord,

None of us enjoys the painful school of discipline, but my confidence is in Your good intention to work this experiential teaching for my good so that I will grow in Christlike character. This brief period of earthly discipline will bring forth the eternal fruit of righteousness.

Amen.

&

Day 102

*Because of the work of the God-man,
I have been set free from the bondage
caused by the fear of death.*

Since God's children have partaken of flesh and blood,
He too shared in their humanity so that by His death
He might destroy him who holds the power of death,
that is, the devil, and free those who all their lives were
held in slavery by their fear of death.

(Hebrews 2:14-15)

Father,

I thank You that the Lord Jesus has partaken of flesh and
blood, so that through His solidarity with the human
condition and His glorious victory over the bondage of
death, we can be liberated from this slavery and set free to
be God's people of meaning, purpose, and hope.

Amen.

Day 103

*Although our time on this earth is brief,
we will live forever through God's eternal word
of life in us.*

All men are like grass, and all their glory is like the
flower of the field.
The grass withers and the flower fades,
because the breath of the Lord blows on it.
Surely the people are grass.
The grass withers and the flower fades,
but the word of our God stands forever.

(Isaiah 40:6-8)

Eternal God,

Your living word endures forever while the generations
of men come and go like waves on the seashore.
Human glory is brief, but divine glory will never
fade. May I embrace, learn, love, and obey Your life-
giving Word in my life, and may I reproduce your Word
in others.

Amen.

Day 104

*In Christ, I share in the blessings
and benefits of the new covenant.*

When You promised to make a new covenant
with the house of Israel,
You said, "I will put My law within them and
write it on their hearts.
I will be their God, and they will be My people.
No longer will each one teach his neighbor,
or each one his brother, saying,
'Know the Lord,' because they shall all know Me,
from the least of them to the greatest of them.
For I will forgive their iniquity and will remember
their sins no more."

(Jeremiah 31:33-34)

Lord,

The beauty and holiness of Your law is beyond human attainment, but because Christ dwells in me, He can live His life through me. May I invite Him to do this each day, so that I will truly know you and walk before You in ways that are pleasing and honoring to You.

Amen.

Day 105

The Lord is utterly dependable in all the circumstances of life.

The Lord upholds all who fall and lifts up all
who are bowed down.
The eyes of all look to You,
and You give them their food at the proper time.
You open Your hand and satisfy the desire of
every living thing.

(Psalm 145:14-16)

O Lord,

I am grateful that I can always look to You with confidence and expectant hope. You know my needs and circumstances, and You continually know and desire what is best for me. I ask for the grace of increasing confidence in Your benevolence and power.

Amen.

Day 106

The living and all-powerful Lord of all creation invites me to enjoy the rich pleasures of being with Him and knowing Him.

The Lord said, "Behold, I stand at the door and knock.
If anyone hears My voice and opens the door,
I will come in to him and dine with him,
and he with Me.
To him who overcomes, I will give the right to
sit with Me on My throne,
just as I overcame and sat down with My Father
on His throne."

(Revelation 3:20-21)

Lord Jesus,

You have overcome the power of sin and of death, and You invite me to welcome You into my innermost being where I can commune with You. I ask for the grace to be an overcomer through Your indwelling power, so that I will have the right to sit with You on Your throne.

Amen.

Day 107

*The Lord Jesus will come again with power
and great glory to reign over all the earth.*

As the lightning comes from the east and
flashes to the west,
so will be the coming of the Son of Man.
The sign of the Son of Man will appear in the sky,
and all the nations of the earth will mourn,
and they will see the Son of Man coming on the clouds
of the sky with power and great glory.

(Matthew 24:27, 30)

Lord Christ,

My firm confidence and expectant hope is in You and
in Your glorious promises. I look forward to the
consummation of history when You come to establish the
fullness of Your kingdom upon the earth. Your kingdom
come, Your will be done, on earth as it is in heaven.

Amen.

Day 108

*The God who called us
will also keep us in His loving grip.*

I am confident of this,
that He who began a good work in me
will carry it on to completion until the day
of Christ Jesus.

(Philippians 1:6)

O Lord,

I am glad of the assurance in Your Word that You complete what You have begun. Thank You for choosing and calling me and giving me new life in Christ Jesus, and also for Your promise that You will keep me for the day of redemption when I enter into Your glorious presence.

Amen.

Day 109

*When I received Christ,
I entered into God's eternal family as
a beloved child.*

As many as received Christ,
to them He gave the right to become children of God,
to those who believe in His name,
who were born not of blood,
nor of the will of the flesh,
nor of the will of man, but of God.

(John 1:12-13)

Lord Jesus,

I have transferred my trust from myself to You and have received Your free gift of forgiveness and of eternal life. Because of Your gift, I have the assurance that I have become a child of God through the second birth that comes from above.

Amen.

᪥

Day 110

God is the ever-present and all-sufficient
Savior and deliverer of all who take refuge in Him.

The Lord is my rock and my fortress and my deliverer;
my God is my rock; I will take refuge in Him,
my shield and the horn of my salvation,
my stronghold and my refuge — my Savior,
You save me from violence.
I call on the Lord, who is worthy of praise,
and I am saved from my enemies.

(2 Samuel 22:2-4)

Lord God,

You alone are my hope and shield and place of refuge.
I have entered into Your stronghold and in that quiet
place I discover Your presence, peace, and power in spite
of the uncertainties and tempests of this earthly life. I
will call upon You and give You praise, for You alone are
worthy.

Amen.

Day 111

The Lord is ever-present to strengthen,
help, and protect those who call upon Him.

I will not fear, for You are with me;
I will not be dismayed, for You are my God.
You will strengthen me and help me;
You will uphold me with Your righteous right hand.
For You are the Lord my God,
who takes hold of my right hand and says to me,
"Do not fear; I will help you."

(Isaiah 41:10, 13)

Dear Lord,

It is with gratitude and confidence in Your many mercies that I call upon You in times of peace and times of distress. You have taken hold of my right hand and told me not to fear, for You will help me. Therefore I will not be dismayed or lose hope.

Amen.

Day 112

God has equipped me and empowered me to walk in the new nature I have received in Christ.

God's divine power has given me all things
that pertain to life and godliness,
through the knowledge of Him who called
me by His own glory and virtue.
Through these He has given me His very great
and precious promises,
so that through them I may be a partaker
of the divine nature,
having escaped the corruption that is in the
world by lust.

(2 Peter 1:3-4)

Lord,

It is through Your power that I have become a partaker of the divine nature, having received the gift of Christ's indwelling life. You have called me to this through Your glory and goodness, and granted me the unbounded riches of Your great and precious promises.

Amen.

Day 113

*When I live and abide in the love of Jesus,
I desire to obey His command to love
God and others.*

As the Father has loved You, You also have loved me.
I must abide in Your love.
If I keep Your commandments, I will abide in Your love,
just as You kept Your Father's commandments
and abide in His love.
You have told me this so that Your joy may be in me
and that my joy may be full.

(John 15:9-11)

Lord Jesus,

May I revel in Your loving presence and abide in Your love by living in obedience to the things You command me to do. May I practice Your presence in all of my activities and relationships so that Your joy will become ever more full in my life.

Amen.

‰

Day 114

Because I believe in Jesus,
I rejoice in the living hope that
I will see Him soon.

Though I have not seen Jesus, I love Him;
and though I do not see Him now but believe in Him,
I rejoice with joy inexpressible and full of glory,
for I am receiving the end of my faith, the
salvation of my soul.

(1 Peter 1:8-9)

Father,

You have graced me with a love for Jesus even though I have not yet seen Him. I will continue to hope and trust in Him in this life, knowing that in the life to come I will see Him face to face. In this I rejoice as I await the fullness of my salvation in that glorious day.

Amen.

Day 115

*When we walk in the light of God's presence,
we are exalted in His righteousness.*

Blessed are those who have learned to acclaim You,
who walk in the light of Your presence, O Lord.
They rejoice in Your name all day long,
and they are exalted in Your righteousness.

(Psalm 89:15-16)

Lord God,

May I rejoice in Your name throughout the day and order my steps as if I could see You. Let me walk in the light of Your presence and learn to acclaim You in thought, word, and deed. Then I will be exalted in Your righteousness, and my joy will continue to increase.

Amen.

Day 116

*In Christ, I am destined to receive
a kingdom that cannot be shaken.*

Since I am receiving a kingdom that cannot be shaken,
I will be thankful and so worship God acceptably
with reverence and awe,
for my God is a consuming fire.

(Hebrews 12:28-29)

My God,

I want to worship You acceptably with reverence and awe, for You are a consuming fire of holiness and love. Teach me to be ever more thankful, so that growing gratitude will be my worship as I remember Your radiant promise that I am destined in Christ to receive a kingdom that can never be overthrown or diminished.

Amen.

Day 117

*Since I am in Christ, God has implanted
His light, glory, and power within me.*

God who said, "Let light shine out of darkness"
made His light shine in my heart
to give me the light of the knowledge of the glory
of God in the face of Christ.
But I have this treasure in an earthen vessel
to show that this all-surpassing power is
from God and not from me.

(2 Corinthians 4:6-7)

O God,

Although I was formerly darkness, now I am light in the Lord. You have given me the light of the knowledge of Your glory in the face of Your Son, and this treasure becomes most evident when I walk in dependence on Your power and not on my own.

Amen.

Day 118

Because I believe in the name of the Son of God,
I know that I have eternal life.

God has given me eternal life, and this life is in His Son.
He who has the Son has life;
he who does not have the Son of God does not have life.
Since I believe in the name of the Son of God,
I know that I have eternal life.

(1 John 5:11-13)

Lord God,

I thank You for the boundless and costly gift of eternal
life that was purchased by the redemptive work of
Your Son. Since I have come to believe in His name, I have
Your assurance that I have eternal life in Him. May I live
and walk in His life and display it to others.

Amen.

Day 119

*Since the Lord is the strength of my life,
I need fear no one.*

The Lord is my light and my salvation;
whom shall I fear?
The Lord is the strength of my life;
of whom shall I be afraid?

(Psalm 27:1)

O Lord,

You are my light and my salvation, and it is in You that my real strength resides. Because of Your empowering presence, I will not be fearful or dismayed. When I am anxious, I will turn my burdens over to You and replace earthly fear with divine peace.

Amen.

Day 120

When I approach You by asking,
seeking, and knocking,
I have Your assurance that You will respond.

When I ask, it will be given to me;
when I seek, I will find;
when I knock, the door will be opened to me.
For everyone who asks receives; he who seeks finds;
and to him who knocks, the door will be opened.

(Matthew 7:7-8; Luke 11:9-10)

Lord,

I come to You in full acknowledgement of my desperation and need for You. I am grateful that You open the door upon which I knock, and that You reward those who seek You. In Your grace You give me better than what I request, because You alone know what I truly need.

Amen.

Day 121

*I can be confident that God will answer
my prayers when I trust in Him.*

You have said, "Whatever you ask for in prayer,
believe that you have received it, and it will be yours."

(Mark 11:24)

Lord,

May I walk in Your will and desire the things You
desire for me. I will delight myself in You and ask
without wavering in doubt and disbelief, trusting in Your
boundless resources and in Your willingness to give me
what is best.

Amen.

Day 122

*In Christ, I have a source of peace
that the world cannot give.*

Peace You leave with me; Your peace You give to me.
Not as the world gives, do You give to me.
I will not let my heart be troubled nor let it be fearful.

(John 14:27)

Dear Lord,

I will revel and rejoice in the transcendent peace that You alone can give to me. Because I have hoped and trusted in Jesus, I need never be troubled and fearful. You have given me an inner peace that the world can neither understand nor offer.

Amen.

Day 123

Having confessed and believed in the Lord Jesus,
I am saved and will never be put to shame.

If I confess with my mouth the Lord Jesus
and believe in my heart that God raised Him
from the dead, I will be saved.
For it is with my heart that I believe unto righteousness,
and it is with my mouth that I confess unto salvation.
As the Scripture says, "Whoever trusts in Him
will not be put to shame."

(Romans 10:9-11)

Lord Jesus,

I have trusted in You with my heart and confessed You before others with my mouth. Knowing that You are wholly trustworthy, I will never be put to shame, but continue on the way of righteousness and salvation until I stand before You, holy and blameless.

Amen.

Day 124

*God fully provides for all my needs
according to His glorious riches in Christ Jesus.*

God will supply all my needs according to His
glorious riches in Christ Jesus.
To my God and Father be glory
for ever and ever.

(Philippians 4:19-20)

Father,

My hope for every form of provision—physical,
emotional, relational, financial—is solely founded
on Your promises and power. You fully know me and all
of my needs, and I look with confidence to Your abundant
provision of every good thing that will lead to life and
godliness.

Amen.

Day 125

The God who is there rewards those who earnestly seek Him.

Without faith it is impossible to please God,
for he who comes to Him must believe that He exists,
and that He is a rewarder of those
who earnestly seek Him.

(Hebrews 11:6)

Lord God,

May I please You through a growing faith and confidence in Your goodness, greatness, grace, and glory. Not only do You exist, but You are the source of all that is. I will earnestly seek You, knowing that You always reward those who pursue You.

Amen.

❦

Day 126

*In Christ, I am destined to receive
a glorified resurrection body.*

My citizenship is in heaven, from which I also
eagerly await a Savior,
the Lord Jesus Christ, who will transform
my lowly body
and conform it to His glorious body,
according to the exertion of His ability to subject all
things to Himself.

(Philippians 3:20-21)

Lord,

I eagerly look forward to the coming of the Lord
Jesus Christ, who will subject all things in the created
order to Himself. In that day, I will receive a resurrected
body that will be glorious and perfect, because it will be
conformed to Jesus' glorious body.

Amen.

Day 127

*God is our refuge and fortress,
and we can rest in Him.*

He who dwells in the shelter of the Most High
will rest in the shadow of the Almighty.
I will say of the Lord, "He is my refuge and my fortress,
my God, in whom I trust."

(Psalm 91:1-2)

Lord God Almighty,

I thank You that You have become my refuge and fortress, and that I can rest in the shadow of the Almighty. You are the Most High, the Almighty, the Lord, and my God in whom I trust. I will not be fearful but confident, knowing that nothing can separate me from Your love and power.

Amen.

Day 128

*As a member of God's flock, I have the
gift of eternal life,
and no one can snatch me from the Father's grip.*

Your sheep hear Your voice, and You know them,
and they follow You.
You give them eternal life, and they shall never perish;
no one can snatch them out of Your hand.
The Father, who has given them to You,
is greater than all;
no one can snatch them out of the Father's hand.

(John 10:27-29)

Father,

By Your grace, I have heard Your voice and am a member of Your flock. You have given me eternal life, and I will never perish or be separated from You. You hold me in Your hand, and I delight to follow You.

Amen.

Day 129

*The Spirit of God who raised Jesus from the dead
lives in me and will raise me from the dead.*

If Christ is in me, my body is dead because of sin,
yet my spirit is alive because of righteousness.
And if the Spirit of Him who raised Jesus
from the dead is living in me,
He who raised Christ from the dead
will also give life to my mortal body through
His Spirit, who lives in me.

(Romans 8:10-11)

Lord,

I give thanks that though my body is mortal, yet my spirit is alive with the indwelling Holy Spirit. And it is through the power of Your Holy Spirit that I will be raised from the dead so that I will be made complete in my spirit, soul, and body.

Amen.

Day 130

The Holy Spirit has been given to me
as a guarantee
that my mortality will be swallowed up by life.

I know that if my earthly house, or tent, is destroyed,
I have a building from God, a house not made with
hands, eternal in the heavens.
For in this house I groan, longing to be clothed
with my heavenly dwelling,
because when I am clothed, I will not be found naked.
For while I am in this tent, I groan, being burdened,
because I do not want to be unclothed but to be clothed,
so that what is mortal may be swallowed up by life.
Now it is God who has made me for this very purpose
and has given me the Spirit as a guarantee.

(2 Corinthians 5:1-5)

O Lord,

I groan in my mortal corruption, knowing that my
earthly body is frail and temporary. I await the day
when I will be clothed with an eternal dwelling that will
display Your glory and will never be corrupted or
diminished.

Amen.

Day 131

When I abide in Jesus, I experience the joy of answered prayer.

If I abide in You, and Your words abide in me,
I can ask whatever I wish, and it will be done for me.
As I ask in Your name, I will receive,
that my joy may be full.

(John 15:7, 16:24)

Lord Jesus

I know that when I abide in You and let Your words abide in me, the things I desire are also the things that You would be pleased to grant. In these times I can approach You with confidence, knowing that I will receive what I ask in Your name.

Amen.

ॐ

Day 132

*Faith is the victory that overcomes the world,
and my faith is in the person and work
of the Son of God.*

Everyone who believes that Jesus is the
Christ is born of God,
and everyone who loves the Father loves Him
who is begotten of Him.
Whatever is born of God overcomes the world,
and this is the victory that has overcome
the world—our faith.
Who is he who overcomes the world,
but he who believes that Jesus is the Son of God?

(1 John 5:1, 4-5)

Father,

I have come to believe that Jesus is the Christ, Your only
begotten Son. This is the faith that empowers me to
overcome the world. In Him I have received the new
birth and I have come to love You and Your Son.

Amen.

Day 133

*My security is in the Lord
who will bring me safely to
His heavenly kingdom.*

The Lord will deliver me from every evil work
and will bring me safely to His heavenly kingdom.
To Him be glory forever and ever.

(2 Timothy 4:18)

Lord,

My confidence rests entirely on You and not myself.
I know that You will deliver me from all evil
intentions and devices, and that You will bring me safely
in the end to Your heavenly kingdom. There I will behold
Your resplendent glory forever.

Amen.

Day 134

***The Lord is preparing joys
beyond earthly imagination for
those who love Him.***

Eye has not seen, ear has not heard,
nor have entered the heart of man
the things that God has prepared for those
who love Him.

(1 Corinthians 2:9)

Dear God,

I do not possess the mental capacity to begin to imagine what You are preparing to give to Your children. The greatest beauties that I have seen or heard or read about are as nothing in comparison to the eternal ecstasy of being immersed in Your triune glory.

Amen.

Day 135

*The worst pains I will experience in this life
are as nothing in comparison
to the glory that is to come.*

Since I am a child of God, I am an heir of God
and a joint heir with Christ,
if indeed I share in His sufferings in order that I
may also share in His glory.
For I consider that the sufferings of this present time
are not worth comparing with the glory that
will be revealed to me.

(Romans 8:17-18)

O Lord,

This brief earthly existence is fraught with hardships
and disappointments, but I know that even these will
contribute to the glory to come. As a joint heir with Christ,
I will receive that which will endure forever and will
never fade away.

Amen.

Day 136

*In Christ I have a living hope
of an unfading inheritance.*

Blessed be the God and Father of my
Lord Jesus Christ, who according to His
great mercy has given me new birth
into a living hope through the resurrection
of Jesus Christ from the dead,
and into an inheritance that is
incorruptible and undefiled
and unfading, reserved in heaven for me.

(1 Peter 1:3-4)

Father God,

I bless You indeed because of Your great mercy and because of my new birth into a living hope. In Christ, my inheritance will never be corrupted, defiled, or diminished. It is reserved in heaven for me, and I will enjoy the blessings of Your presence in the ages to come.

Amen.

Day 137

God has plans to give me a future and a hope.

"I know the plans I have for you," declares the Lord,
"plans to prosper you and not to harm you,
plans to give you a future and a hope."

(Jeremiah 29:11)

O Lord,

I give thanks that You are my unchanging source of
meaning and hope, and that I am here for a purpose.
Because of Your great love, and because You are in control
of all things, nothing will defeat Your gracious plans to
give me a future and a hope.

Amen.

Day 138

*God is the help of my countenance
and the restorer of my soul.*

Why are you downcast, O my soul?
Why are you disturbed within me?
Hope in God, for I will yet praise Him for the
help of His presence.
O my God, my soul is downcast within me;
therefore I will remember You.
Why are you downcast, O my soul?
Why are you disturbed within me?
Hope in God, for I will yet praise Him,
the help of my countenance and my God.

(Psalm 42:5-6, 11)

Lord God,

When I am downcast and disturbed, may I quickly turn to You and hold fast to Your perfect character. May I practice Your presence in all things and at all times, so that I will walk in Your peace and power in trying times. I will praise You for the help of Your presence.

Amen.

Day 139

The more I walk in loving obedience to Jesus,
the greater my fellowship with
the Father and the Son.

He who has Your commandments and obeys them,
he is the one who loves You;
and he who loves You will be loved by Your Father,
and You will love him and manifest Yourself to him.

(John 14:21)

Lord Jesus,

I ask for the grace to respond to Your Word with a heart of obedience that is prompted by love. I desire a growing manifestation of You and the Father in my life, and I wish to walk in responsiveness to all that You desire me to be and to do.

Amen.

Day 140

*As I delight myself in Your Word,
I will bear roots below and fruit above.*

Blessed is the man who does not walk in
the counsel of the wicked
or stand in the way of sinners or sit
in the seat of scorners.
But his delight is in the law of the Lord,
and in His law he meditates day and night.
And he shall be like a tree planted by
streams of water, which yields its fruit in its season
and whose leaf does not wither;
and whatever he does will prosper.

(Psalm 1:1-3)

Lord,

It is a blessed thing to drink deeply from the well of Your Word and to meditate on Your timeless truths and life-giving precepts. I want to turn away from the falsehoods of this world, plant myself in Your living Word, and bear the fruit of righteousness.

Amen.

Day 141

*My life is hidden with Christ in God,
and I will appear with Him in glory.*

Since I have been raised with Christ,
I should seek the things above,
where Christ is seated at the right hand of God.
I will set my mind on the things above,
not on the things on the earth,
for I died, and my life is now hidden with Christ in God.
When Christ who is my life appears,
then I also will appear with Him in glory.

(Colossians 3:1-4)

Lord Christ,

You are in me, and I am in You. I choose to believe that I am seated at the right hand of the Father with You, even though this is contrary to my feelings and experiences. In this life I walk by faith, but the day is coming when I will appear with You in glory.

Amen.

ॐ

Day 142

*I have confidence that I will receive
whatever I ask that is according to
the will of Jesus.*

This is the confidence I have in the Son of God,
that if I ask anything according to His will, He hears me.
And if I know that He hears me, whatever I ask,
I know that I have the requests that I have
asked from Him.

(1 John 5:14-15)

Lord Jesus,

May my prayers be in accordance with Your will, so
that I will grow in grace and in intimacy with You.
I give thanks for answered prayer, knowing that You care
about the things that concern me and that You are pleased
when I come to You with my requests.

Amen.

Wisdom

"Christianity
is a statement which,
if false, is of no importance,
and, if true, of infinite importance.
The one thing it cannot be
is moderately important."

– C. S. Lewis, *God in the Dock*

Introduction to Wisdom

If we unthinkingly take life for granted and lose our sense of wonder at God and His creation, our capacity to worship will atrophy. David's ongoing amazement and wonder is captured in Psalm 139, a beautiful meditation on the knowledge, presence, power, and holiness of the Ruler of all creation.

The Word of God calls us to view the world and all of life from a divine rather than a human perspective. Our final integration point and source of meaning is upward, not downward, heavenly, not earthly, the Creator, not the cosmos. The world would define us by default; do nothing, and it will fill your eyes and ears with its system of values. The Word will only define us by discipline; we must choose to sit under its daily tutelage, or our minds will never be renewed and transformed by eternal values.

We were born to worship God. In his book, *Desiring God*, John Piper modifies the Shorter Catechism's answer to the question, "What is the chief end of man?" For him, the chief end of man is to glorify God *by* enjoying Him forever. We honor God most when His glory becomes our greatest pleasure; we worship God best when we pursue our joy in Him above all.

God's loyal love and faithfulness should be the cause of childlike wonder and awe, but for most believers, these have become religious platitudes, mere words that no longer grip their hearts or imaginations. It is easy to lose our first love and forget what we were before we knew Christ and what we would be without Him. Ask God for the grace to make you a worshipper; one who is amazed by His steadfast love and astonished by His faithfulness. Nourish your heart on high thoughts of God through devotional reading of the Scriptures, and worship Him in Spirit and truth.

Any good that takes first place in our hearts is an idol if it is not the Supreme Good, the living God. We were created to have a relationship with Him, and no other person, possession, or position will satisfy our deepest longings.

Day 143

SEEK GOD'S APPROVAL

Should you then seek great things for yourself?
Seek them not.

(Jeremiah 45:5)

Am I now trying to win the approval of people,
or of God?
Or am I trying to please people?
If I were still trying to please people,
I would not be a servant of Christ.

(Galatians 1:10)

Lord God,

I thank You that You have given me acceptability and
worth in Christ. Teach me to enjoy the opportunities
You have given me rather than cramming my schedule in
a quest to merit the acceptance of others. May I be
concerned about pleasing You rather than impressing
people.

Amen.

Day 144

DEMONSTRATE GOD'S KINDNESS TO OTHERS

What is desirable in a person is to show kindness,
and a poor person is better than a liar.

(Proverbs 19:22)

As those who have been chosen of God, holy and
beloved, clothe yourselves with a heart of compassion,
kindness, humility, gentleness, and patience,
bearing with one other and forgiving one other
even as the Lord forgave you;
and above all these things, put on love,
which is the bond of perfection.

(Colossians 3:12-14)

Lord,

Grant me the grace to live in the realization that I have
been called to serve others and not myself. I ask for a
heart of compassion, kindness, humility, gentleness, and
patience in the way I relate to other people. Since I have
been chosen and beloved by You, the living God, may I
demonstrate love and kindness to others.

Amen.

Day 145

LOOK TO GOD FOR WISDOM

The fear of the Lord is the beginning of knowledge,
but fools despise wisdom and discipline.

(Proverbs 1:7)

The Lord gives wisdom;
from His mouth comes knowledge and understanding.
He stores up sound wisdom for the upright;
He is a shield to those who live with integrity,
guarding the paths of justice and protecting the way of
His saints. Then you will understand righteousness
and justice and honesty—every good path.
For wisdom will enter your heart,
and knowledge will be pleasant to your soul. Discretion
will protect you, and understanding will guard you.

(Proverbs 2:6-11)

O Lord,

You alone are the wellspring of knowledge and
wisdom. May I diligently seek You and order my
steps with integrity, righteousness, justice, and honesty. I
ask that Your wisdom will permeate my heart and
practice, and that I will grow in the skill of living with each
aspect of my life under Your dominion.

Amen.

Day 146

BE QUICK TO HEAR AND SLOW TO SPEAK

Everyone should be quick to hear, slow to speak, and slow to anger, for the anger of man does not produce the righteousness of God.

(James 1:19-20)

In a multitude of words, transgression is inevitable, but he who restrains his lips is wise.

(Proverbs 10:19)

A fool takes no pleasure in understanding, but only in airing his own opinions.

(Proverbs 18:2)

Lord God,

I ask for the wisdom to restrain my speech and the patience to listen more carefully to others before responding with my own opinions. May I be a gracious and others-centered listener rather than a controlling and self-centered talker. I desire to serve others by listening, caring, and encouraging.

Amen.

157

Day 147

RESPOND CORRECTLY TO REPROOF

The person who listens to a life-giving rebuke
will be at home among the wise.
The one who refuses correction despises himself,
but whoever heeds reproof gains understanding.

(Proverbs 15:31-32)

A rebuke goes deeper into a wise person
than a hundred lashes into a fool.

(Proverbs 17:10)

Lord,

Although there is no pleasure in being rebuked and corrected, I desire a teachable spirit that is willing to receive the truth in humility. May I listen for the truth and not filter it out through stubbornness and defensiveness, so that I will grow in wisdom and make the necessary mid-course corrections that will lead to maturity in character.

Amen.

Day 148

FLEE FROM THE LOVE OF MONEY

The one who loves money will not be satisfied with money;
nor he who loves abundance, with its increase.

(Ecclesiastes 5:10)

Those who want to get rich fall into temptation and a snare
and into many foolish and harmful desires
that plunge people into ruin and destruction.
For the love of money is a root of all kinds of evil,
and some by longing for it have wandered from the faith
and pierced themselves with many sorrows.
But I will flee from these things, and pursue righteousness,
godliness, faith, love, patience, and gentleness.

(1 Timothy 6:9-11)

Lord God,

I want to give my life in exchange for the things You declare to be important rather than the things that are passing away. Grant me the grace to turn away from the lure of worldly wealth, since I know that it will never satisfy my soul, but will draw me away from You. You are my true source of provision and security, and I will look to You and not to the world for these needs.

Amen.   159

Day 149

TRUST IN GOD, NOT IN PEOPLE

The fear of man brings a snare,
but he who trusts in the Lord is set on high.

(Proverbs 29:25)

Cursed is the one who trusts in man,
who depends on flesh for his strength
and whose heart turns away from the Lord.
But blessed is the man who trusts in the Lord,
whose confidence is in Him.

(Jeremiah 17:5, 7)

Lord,

I ask for the wisdom to trust in You entirely and exclusively and not to put my hope and trust in people above You. I will depend upon You for my strength and place my confidence in Your promises, and in this way I will avoid the snare of fearing people's opinions more than Your truth.

Amen.

ॐ

Day 150

CONSIDER THE GOOD OF OTHERS

We who are strong ought to bear the weaknesses
of those who are not strong, and not to please ourselves.
Each of us should please his neighbor for his good,
to build him up.

(Romans 15:1-2)

No one should seek his own good,
but the good of others.

(1 Corinthians 10:24)

Father,

Because You have given me an unchanging foundation
for identity, significance, and worth, may I embrace
this truth and act upon it by serving others rather than
using them. May I bear the weaknesses of others and
desire to serve others by seeking their good. Since You
have sought my good, I have been liberated to do the
same for others.

Amen.

Day 151

INVEST IN LASTING RELATIONSHIPS

The sons of this world are more shrewd
in dealing with their own kind than are the sons of light.
I would be wise to use worldly wealth
to make friends for myself, so that when it is gone,
they may welcome me into the eternal dwellings.

(Luke 16:8-9)

What is my hope or joy or crown of rejoicing
in the presence of the Lord Jesus at His coming?
My glory and joy is the people
in whose lives I have been privileged to have a ministry.

(1 Thessalonians 2:19-20)

Lord God,

Grant me the grace of an eternal perspective so that I
will treat people in light of eternity. I ask for the
wisdom of investing the resources You have entrusted to
me in the lives of people—immortal beings You have put
in my path. May I give my life in exchange for that which
can never be lost or corrupted.

Amen.

162

Day 152

LIVE WITH THE END IN VIEW

Direct my footsteps according to Your word,
and let no iniquity have dominion over me.

(Psalm 119:133)

The hour has come for me to wake up from sleep,
for my salvation is nearer now than when
I first believed.
The night is nearly over; the day is almost here.
Therefore I will cast off the works of darkness
and put on the armor of light.

(Romans 13:11-12)

O Lord,

May I live out my days with an eye to the end of my earthly endeavors so that I will treasure the things You have declared to be important rather than the things the world urges me to seek. I want to cast off the works of darkness, order my footsteps according to Your word, and put on the armor of light.

Amen.

Day 153

WALK IN HUMILITY

Before his downfall the heart of a man is haughty,
but humility comes before honor.

(Proverbs 18:12)

Blessed are the poor in spirit,
for theirs is the kingdom of heaven.
Blessed are those who mourn,
for they will be comforted.
Blessed are the meek,
for they will inherit the earth.

(Matthew 5:3-5)

Dear Lord,

I ask for the grace of growing realization of my true
condition before You. May I focus on Your glory,
goodness, and grace, and not on myself. Then I will more
clearly grasp my poverty of spirit and mourn over my
foolish pride. I would live in humility and meekness
rather than self-assertion and the human quest for power.

Amen.

Day 154

CULTIVATE A HEART FOR THE HARVEST

The harvest is plentiful, but the workers are few.
Therefore, I will pray that the Lord of the harvest
will send out workers into His harvest.

(Matthew 9:37-38; Luke 10:2)

Do you not say, "Four months more and then comes the
harvest"? Behold, I say to you, lift up your eyes
and look at the fields, for they are white for harvest.
Even now the reaper draws his wages,
and gathers fruit for eternal life, that he who sows and
he who reaps may rejoice together.

(John 4:35-36)

O Lord,

Please give me eyes for the harvest and a heart for
evangelism so that I will long to see the people I love
come into a saving relationship with You through the
merits and grace of Your Son, Jesus Christ. May I be
involved in the harvest as a worker who prepares the soil,
plants the seed of Your word, cultivates the soil, and waits
for Your harvest.

Amen.

165

Day 155

PRACTICE INTEGRITY IN YOUR WORK

I will have accurate and honest standards
in my business practices.

(Deuteronomy 25:15)

He who walks in integrity walks securely,
but he who perverts his way will be found out.

(Proverbs 10:9)

Dear God,

I want to live each day with the integrity of harmonizing
my inward thought life with my outward practice, so
that my words and my works will point to the power and
presence of Your life in me. May I manifest this integrity in
all the details of my career so that the so-called secular
becomes spiritual.

Amen.

Day 156

LIVE IN HOLINESS
AND HOPE

I want the Lord to establish my heart
as blameless and holy before our God and Father
at the coming of our Lord Jesus with all His saints.

(1 Thessalonians 3:13)

I desire to be diligent to realize the full
assurance of hope to the end.
I do not want to become sluggish
but to imitate those who through faith and
patience inherit the promises.

(Hebrews 6:11-12)

Lord,

Please establish my heart as blameless and holy before
You through the transforming work of Christ in me,
the hope of glory. May I be diligent to walk in this hope
and to persevere to the end with faith, trust, and patience
as I await the fullness of Your promises.

Amen.

Day 157

GUARD YOUR THOUGHT LIFE

I will flee from sexual immorality.
All other sins a man commits are outside his body,
but the immoral person sins against his own body.

(1 Corinthians 6:18)

I will consider the members of my earthly body
as dead to immorality, impurity, passion, evil desires,
and greed, which is idolatry.
Because of these, the wrath of God is coming,
and in them I once walked when I lived in them.

(Colossians 3:5-7)

Lord God,

Grant me the power and intention to guard my thought life so that I will not succumb to the baseness of immorality and impurity. I flee to You and away from sensuality and immorality. I choose to live in light of the day when I will give an account to Christ—may I not be ashamed on that day.

Amen.

&

Day 158

LEARN THE SECRET OF CONTENTMENT

I will covet no one's money or possessions.

(Acts 20:33)

Godliness with contentment is great gain.
For I brought nothing into the world, and I can take
nothing out of it. But if I have food and clothing, with
these I will be content.

(1 Timothy 6:6-8)

Dear Lord,

I pray for the gift of contentment, a gift that is rare and precious since it is possessed by so few. May I choose to allow You to determine the content and disposition of my life rather than seeking to determine it myself. Then I will know the secret of contentment as I stop comparing myself with others and revel in the goodness of Your will and plans for me.

Amen.

Day 159

COMMIT YOUR WAYS AND WORKS TO GOD

I will commit my works to the Lord,
and my plans will be established.

(Proverbs 16:3)

I want my conscience to testify that I have
conducted myself in the world
in the holiness and sincerity that are from God,
not in fleshly wisdom but in the grace of God,
especially in my relations with others.

(2 Corinthians 1:12)

Lord,

It is to You that I commit my effort, my hopes, my fears, my dreams, my aspirations, and my deep desires. May I conduct myself in the world in Your holiness, in Your grace, and in Your wisdom, and may I treat the people You have placed in my life with love and charity.

Amen.

Day 160

BECOME WINSOME TO A WATCHING WORLD

I should walk in wisdom toward outsiders,
making the most of every opportunity.
My speech should always be with grace,
seasoned with salt,
so that I may know how to answer each person.

(Colossians 4:5-6)

I will sanctify Christ as Lord in my heart,
always being ready to make a defense
to everyone who asks me to give the reason for the hope
that is in me,
but with gentleness and respect.

(1 Peter 3:15)

Lord God,

I want to sanctify Christ as Lord in my heart and seek His honor. May I live with such quality that people who observe me will want an explanation for the hope that they observe in me. When I have opportunities to share the Good News to others, give me wisdom, clarity, and boldness so that the gospel will be credible.

Amen.

Day 161

FOLLOW THE PATH OF THE RIGHTEOUS

Who may ascend the hill of the Lord?
Who may stand in His holy place?
He who has clean hands and a pure heart,
who has not lifted up his soul to an idol
or sworn by what is false.

(Psalm 24:3-4)

The path of the righteous is like the first gleam of dawn,
shining ever brighter until the full light of day.
But the way of the wicked is like darkness;
they do not know what makes them stumble.

(Proverbs 4:18-19)

Dear God,

I ask that I will walk in the path of the righteous in the light of Your guidance and truth. I seek to ascend the hill of Your presence and commune with You in the holy places of Christlike character and goodness. Give me the grace of holy desire to be more and more like Jesus.

Amen.

∾

Day 162

WALK AS A CHILD OF LIGHT

Come, my children, listen to me; I will teach you the fear
of the Lord. Who is the man who desires life
and loves many days that he may see good?
Keep your tongue from evil and your lips from speaking
guile. Depart from evil and do good; seek peace and
pursue it. The eyes of the Lord are on the righteous,
and His ears are attentive to their cry.

(Psalm 34:11-15)

I was once darkness, but now I am light in the Lord.
I will walk as a child of light
(for the fruit of the light consists in all goodness and
righteousness and truth),
learning what is pleasing to the Lord.

(Ephesians 5:8-10)

Lord,

As a child of the light I will, by Your grace, walk in the
light of Your presence and love. I want to live in the
fear of the Lord, to guard my speech, and to make
choices that are pleasing and honoring to You, so that I
will bear the enduring fruit of goodness and
righteousness and truth.

Amen.   173

Day 163

GROW IN LOVE WITH THE LORD

Father in heaven, hallowed be Your name.
Your kingdom come;
Your will be done on earth as it is in heaven.

(Matthew 6:9-10)

Though I have not seen Jesus, I love Him;
and though I do not see Him now but believe in Him,
I rejoice with joy inexpressible and full of glory,
for I am receiving the end of my faith,
the salvation of my soul.

(1 Peter 1:8-9)

Father,

May Your holy name be lifted up and honored. I warmly anticipate the fullness of Your kingdom as I await the coming of the Lord Jesus. Though I have not yet seen Him, I love Him and rejoice with glorious joy that I will commune with You, with Your Son, and with Your Holy Spirit in the ages to come.

Amen.

Day 164

GUARD YOUR SPEECH

I will put away perversity from my mouth
and keep corrupt talk far from my lips.

(Proverbs 4:24)

I will not let any corrupt word come out of my mouth,
but only what is helpful for building others up
according to their needs, that it may
impart grace to those who hear.

(Ephesians 4:29)

Lord,

I need the wisdom of placing a guard about my speech,
so that my words will encourage, edify, and exhort
rather than dishearten, hurt, and alienate others. May I
monitor what I say and think carefully before talking, so
that my words would impart kindness, grace, and good
counsel to those who hear.

Amen.

Day 165

LOVE THE VIRTUE OF HUMILITY

When pride comes, then comes dishonor,
but with humility comes wisdom.

(Proverbs 11:2)

The proud looks of man will be humbled,
and the loftiness of men brought low;
the Lord alone will be exalted.

(Isaiah 2:11)

O Lord,

I am painfully aware of the proud looks and loftiness of men. May I not become guilty of becoming like what I hate seeing in others. I ask for a spirit of gentleness and humility that seeks to honor and exalt You rather than build myself up in the sight of others.

Amen.

Day 166

PRACTICE THE COURAGE OF OBEDIENCE

I will be strong and courageous,
being careful to obey Your word;
I will not turn from it to the right or to the left,
that I may act wisely wherever I go.

(Joshua 1:7)

I will take courage and not be afraid,
for the Lord Jesus is with me.

(Mark 6:50)

Lord Jesus,

I take strength and comfort in the truth that You are ever
with me. May I be courageous in this present darkness
and spiritual warfare so that I will act in obedience to Your
word. I do not want to stray to the right or to the left, but
to stay on the path of wisdom.

Amen.

Day 167

PURSUE A LASTING LEGACY

As we have opportunity, we should do good
to all people, especially to those who belong
to the family of faith.

(Galatians 6:10)

God is not unjust to be forgetful of our work
and the love we have shown toward His name in having
ministered and continuing to minister to the saints.

(Hebrews 6:10)

Dear God,

I know that You are ever mindful of the work and love
that is done in Your name. I pray that I will seek to
minister to the needs of the people You have placed in my
sphere of influence so that I will mediate Your love and
goodness to them and build a lasting legacy.

Amen.

Day 168

HUMBLE YOURSELF BEFORE GOD

I will submit myself to God and resist the devil,
and he will flee from me.
I will humble myself before the Lord,
and He will exalt me.

(James 4:7, 10)

I will humble myself under the mighty hand of God,
that He may exalt me in due time,
casting all my anxiety upon Him,
because He cares for me.

(1 Peter 5:6-7)

Lord,

I submit all that I know of myself to all that I know of You. As I do so, I can stand firm against the schemes of the enemy. I know that humility comes before honor and that You will exalt those who have been faithful to You in due time. Therefore, I humble myself under Your mighty hand and cast all my anxiety upon You.

Amen.

Day 169

BE CONTENT WITH GOD'S PROVISION

I shall not covet my neighbor's house,
my neighbor's wife,
his manservant or maidservant,
his ox or donkey,
or anything that belongs to my neighbor.

(Exodus 20:17; Deuteronomy 5:21)

I will beware and be on my guard against all
covetousness, for my life does not consist in the
abundance of my possessions.

(Luke 12:15)

Lord God,

Protect me, I pray, from the insidious nature of covetousness that would tempt me to question Your goodness and provision and eliminate contentment from my life. I realize that the measure of my life is not defined by the quality of my possessions, but by the quality of my relationship with You.

Amen.

Day 170

STAND FIRM IN THE FAITH

I will be on my guard, stand firm in the faith,
act with courage, and be strong.

(1 Corinthians 16:13)

I will be self-controlled in all things,
endure hardship, do the work of an evangelist,
and fulfill my ministry.

(2 Timothy 4:5)

Lord,

May I be self-controlled in all things and stand firm in the life-giving faith that is centered on the person and promises of the Lord Jesus Christ. In this spiritual warfare, I choose to honor my allegiance to You, to be on my guard, to endure hardship, to be an agent of the gospel, and to fulfill my ministry.

Amen.

Day 171

GROW IN THE FEAR OF GOD

The fear of the Lord, that is wisdom,
and to depart from evil is understanding.

(Job 28:28)

The fear of the Lord is the beginning of wisdom;
all who practice His commandments have a good
understanding. His praise endures forever.

(Psalm 111:10)

Lord God,

I ask that I would learn to live more fully in the awe and
fear of Your holy name. May this be the foundation and
wellspring of true wisdom in my life. I want to cling to
Your truth and gladly obey Your commandments so that
I will grow in wisdom and understanding.

Amen.

ಕಾ

Day 172

NEVER LOOK DOWN ON OTHERS

I will not trust in myself or in my own righteousness,
nor will I view others with contempt.

(Luke 18:9)

I will be of the same mind with others;
I will not be haughty in mind or wise in my own
estimation, but I will associate with the humble.

(Romans 12:16)

Dear Lord,

As I look into the moral mirror of Your word, may I
realize that all that I am and have comes from Your
hand. I wish to trust in You and not in myself. As I grow
in awareness of Your grace, may this become evident
in the way I relate to people—not with arrogance and
contempt, but with humility and loving service.

Amen.

Day 173

PREPARE YOUR MIND FOR ACTION

Since I belong to the day, I will be self-controlled,
putting on the breastplate of faith and love,
and the hope of salvation as a helmet.

(1 Thessalonians 5:8)

I will prepare my mind for action and be self-controlled,
setting my hope fully on the grace to be brought to me
at the revelation of Jesus Christ.

(1 Peter 1:13)

Lord,

I want to prepare my mind for action and be self-controlled, so that my life will be marked by faith, hope, and love. I set my hope completely on the grace that will be fully manifested at the appearance of Jesus Christ. Since I have faith in all that You have done and hope for what You will do, I can walk in Your love today.

Amen.

ଐ

Day 174

TURN YOUR EAR TO WISDOM

I will receive the words of wisdom and treasure her
commands within me, turning my ear to wisdom
and applying my heart to understanding.
If I cry for discernment and lift up my voice for understanding, if I seek her as silver and search for her as for
hidden treasures, then I will understand the fear of the
Lord and find the knowledge of God.

(Proverbs 2:1-5)

The fear of the Lord is the beginning of wisdom,
and the knowledge of the Holy One is understanding.

(Proverbs 9:10)

O God,

May I greatly treasure Your revealed words of wisdom
and apply my heart not only to hear them, but to
apply them in the various facets of my life. I ask for
understanding and discernment, and I want to grow in
the personal and experiential knowledge of You.

Amen.

Day 175

LOVE AND HOLD FAST TO GOD

I want to love the Lord my God, obey His voice, and
hold fast to Him.
For the Lord is my life and the length of my days.

(Deuteronomy 30:20)

I love You, O Lord, my strength.
The Lord is my rock and my fortress and my deliverer;
my God is my rock, in whom I take refuge.
He is my shield and the horn of my salvation, my
stronghold. I call upon the Lord, who is worthy of praise,
and I am saved from my enemies.

(Psalm 18:1-3)

Lord God,

My prayer is to love You, to obey Your voice, and to
hold fast to You as my very life. You are my rock and
my fortress and deliverer, and I take refuge in the
stronghold of Your salvation. You alone are worthy of all
praise, and I call upon Your holy name.

Amen.

Day 176

PUT TRUTH INTO PRACTICE

Has the Lord as much delight in burnt offerings
and sacrifices as in obeying the voice of the Lord?
To obey is better than sacrifice, and to heed is better than
the fat of rams. For rebellion is like the sin of divination,
and stubbornness is as iniquity and idolatry.

(1 Samuel 15:22-23)

I desire not only to call You Lord but to do what You say.
By Your grace, I will come to You, hear Your words, and
put them into practice. Then I will be like a man
building a house, who dug down deep and laid the
foundation on rock, and when a flood came, the torrent
struck that house but could not shake it,
because it was well built.

(Luke 6:46-48)

Dear Lord,

May I hear Your words and receive them by putting
them in practice each day. I want to build upon the
rock of Your truth rather than the sand of my feelings. So
I ask for the empowerment to obey Your revealed word
and to fully carry out what You have commanded, so that
my life will be pleasing to You.

Amen.

Day 177

TRUST UNRESERVEDLY IN GOD

The Lord is my strength and my shield;
my heart trusts in Him, and I am helped.
My heart greatly rejoices,
and I will give thanks to Him in song.

(Psalm 28:7)

I will not let my heart be troubled.
I will trust in God and trust also in Christ.

(John 14:1)

Lord,

During the trials of this life, I will trust wholly in You and in Your Son Jesus Christ. As I do this, I will move from anxiety to peace, and from resentment to gratitude. My heart will greatly rejoice, and I will joyfully give thanks to You, for You are my strength and my shield.

Amen.

∽

Day 178

WALK IN THE POWER OF THE SPIRIT

You have asked the Father,
and He has given me another Comforter to be with me
forever, even the Spirit of truth, whom the world cannot
receive, because it neither sees Him nor knows Him.
But I know Him, for He lives in me.

(John 14:16-17)

I am not in the flesh but in the Spirit,
since the Spirit of God lives in me.
And if anyone does not have the Spirit of Christ,
he does not belong to Him.

(Romans 8:9)

Lord Jesus,

Because of Your finished work on the cross and Your resurrection and ascension to the right hand of the Father, we have received the great gift of the indwelling Comforter, the Spirit of truth. May I walk each day in the power of the Spirit who lives in me, and may He manifest Your abiding life in and through me.

Amen.

Day 179

DRINK THE LIVING WATER

Everyone who drinks ordinary water will be thirsty
again, but whoever drinks the water You give will never
thirst. Indeed, the water You give becomes in us
a spring of water welling up to eternal life.

(John 4:13-14)

Whoever hears the word of Jesus
and believes Him who sent Him
has eternal life and will not come into judgment,
but has passed over from death to life.

(John 5:24)

Lord Jesus,

I have heard Your word and have transferred my hope
and trust to You. Having believed in You, I have
received the gift of Your living water that wells up into
eternal life. Because Your life is in me, I will not come into
a judgment of condemnation. I have been taken out of
death and transferred to the kingdom of new life.

Amen.

Day 180

BE ANXIOUS FOR NOTHING

I will not worry about tomorrow, for tomorrow will
worry about itself. Each day has enough
trouble of its own.

(Matthew 6:34)

I do not want to be worried and troubled about many
things; only one thing is needed.
Like Mary, I want to choose the good part,
which will not be taken away from me.

(Luke 10:41-42)

Lord,

You have given me the power to rise above the fears
and anxieties of this life as I choose to hope and trust
in You and in Your faithful promises. Thank You that I can
choose the good part, the one thing most needful, and that
by putting You above all else, I no longer have to worry or
be consumed by fear.

Amen.

Day 181

BEAR THE FRUIT OF RIGHTEOUSNESS

By this is Your Father glorified,
that I bear much fruit,
showing myself to be Your disciple.

(John 15:8)

Just as I presented the members of my body
as slaves to impurity and to ever-increasing lawlessness,
so I now present my members
as slaves to righteousness, leading to holiness.

(Romans 6:19)

Father,

As one who has been raised from the dead and made alive in Christ, I present myself and the members of my body to You. I want to bear abundant and lasting fruit by abiding in Jesus and proving to be His disciple. May the fruit of the righteousness of Christ in me bring honor and glory to You.

Amen.

— ✍ —

Day 182

EMBRACE THE TRUTH ABOUT YOUR IDENTITY

I do not want to be conformed to the pattern of this world but to be transformed by the renewing of my mind, that I may prove that the will of God is good and acceptable and perfect.

(Romans 12:2)

May the God of my Lord Jesus Christ, the Father of glory, give me a spirit of wisdom and of revelation in the full knowledge of Him, and may the eyes of my heart be enlightened, in order that I may know what is the hope of His calling, what are the riches of His glorious inheritance in the saints, and what is the incomparable greatness of His power toward us who believe.

(Ephesians 1:17-19)

Lord God,

I ask for a spirit of wisdom and of revelation in the personal and experiential knowledge of You, so that the eyes of my heart would be enlightened. I want to grow in realization of the truth about my calling and inheritance and about Your power in my life. May I renew my mind with Your truth and be progressively transformed into the fullness of Your Son.

Amen.

Day 183

BE FAITHFUL IN THE LITTLE THINGS

I will let the fear of the Lord be upon me,
and I will be careful in what I do,
for with the Lord my God
there is no injustice or partiality or bribery.

(2 Chronicles 19:7)

He who is faithful with very little
is also faithful with much,
and whoever is dishonest with very little
will also be dishonest with much.
If one is not faithful in handling worldly wealth,
who will trust him with true riches?
And if one is not faithful with someone else's property,
who will give him property of his own?

(Luke 16:10-12)

Lord,

May I embrace the discipline of fidelity in the small things of life, knowing that they will shape the course of the great things. I want to order my steps in the fear of You—the desire to honor and please You above all else, and the holy fear of displeasing You.

Amen.

Day 184

DILIGENTLY PURSUE WISDOM

Blessed is the man who finds wisdom, and the man
who gains understanding, for its profit is greater
than that of silver, and its gain than fine gold.
She is more precious than jewels,
and nothing I desire can compare with her.
Long life is in her right hand;
in her left hand are riches and honor.
Her ways are pleasant ways, and all her paths are peace.
She is a tree of life to those who embrace her,
and happy are those who hold her fast.

(Proverbs 3:13-18)

He who gets wisdom loves his own soul;
he who keeps understanding will find good.

(Proverbs 19:8)

Dear Lord,

I pray for the gift of growing wisdom and understanding. These come directly from Your hand, and I ask for this tree of life. May I hold tightly to wisdom and walk in her paths so that I will be pleasing to You and fruitful in the good works You have chosen for me to do.

Amen.

Day 185

GRASP THAT ALL THINGS COME FROM GOD

This is the one You esteem:
he who is humble and contrite of spirit,
and who trembles at Your word.

(Isaiah 66:2b)

Who makes me different from anyone else?
And what do I have that I did not receive?
And if I did receive it,
why I should I boast as though I had not received it?

(1 Corinthians 4:7)

Lord,

Grant me the wisdom to tremble at Your word in a spirit of contrition and humility. May I grow in the true realization that everything I have in this world—my abilities, my possessions, my accomplishments, my position, my time—all of these come directly from Your hand. May I be wise enough to live in the understanding that all of life is a gift from You.

Amen.

❧

Day 186

PRACTICE FAITH AND LOVE

I will keep the pattern of sound teaching that I have
heard, in faith and love which are in Christ Jesus.

(2 Timothy 1:13)

I will not love with words or tongue,
but in deed and in truth.
By this I will know that I am of the truth
and will assure my heart before Him;
for if my heart condemns me,
God is greater than my heart, and knows all things.
If my heart does not condemn me,
I have confidence before God
and receive from Him whatever I ask,
because I keep His commandments
and do the things that are pleasing in His sight.

(1 John 3:18-22)

Father,

May my love be sincere and truthful, not in empty
words or lifeless faith. I want to keep the pattern of
sound teaching that I have received and express this in
actions that communicate faith and love. I ask that my life
will one of obedience and faithfulness, so that my heart
will be confident and not condemning.

Amen.

Day 187

TREASURE CHRIST ABOVE ALL ELSE

To me, to live is Christ and to die is gain.

(Philippians 1:21)

Whatever was gain to me I now consider loss
for the sake of Christ.
What is more, I consider all things loss
compared to the surpassing greatness of knowing
Christ Jesus my Lord,
for whose sake I have suffered the loss of all things
and consider them rubbish, that I may gain Christ and
be found in Him, not having a righteousness of my own
that comes from the law,
but that which is through faith in Christ—the
righteousness that comes from God on the basis of faith.

(Philippians 3:7-9)

Lord Jesus,

You are my life, and to die is to be ushered into Your
manifest presence. Nothing this world has to offer can
remotely compare with such a real and abiding treasure.
The basis for my welcome to the Father's household is the
righteousness You have offered by grace through faith.

Amen.

Day 188

SEEK THE LORD'S COMMENDATION

Let him who thinks he stands take heed lest he fall.

(1 Corinthians 10:12)

I do not dare to classify or compare myself with other
people, for it is unwise to measure or compare myself
with others.
I will not boast beyond proper limits
but within the sphere of the gospel of Christ.
"Let him who boasts boast in the Lord."
For it is not the one who commends himself who is
approved, but the one whom the Lord commends.

(2 Corinthians 10:12-14, 17-18)

Lord,

May I boast only in You and not in anything I have or
have done. My identity is based on being, not in
having and doing, and my new being is that of a child of
God. I will boast in the sphere of the gospel of Christ and
in the truth that in Him, condemnation before You has
been replaced by commendation.

Amen.

Day 189

PERSEVERE IN TIMES OF TRIAL

I will consider it all joy whenever I fall
into various trials, knowing that the testing of
my faith produces endurance.
And I will let endurance finish its work, so that I may be
mature and complete, lacking in nothing.

(James 1:2-4)

Blessed is the man who perseveres under trial,
because when he has been approved,
he will receive the crown of life
that God has promised to those who love Him.

(James 1:12)

Dear God,

Though the trials and afflictions of life are painful, I can rejoice in what You seek to accomplish through them. You test and purge and refine me in the fires of adversity so that I will better reflect the image of Your Son. I pray for the grace and power to persevere so that I will grow in endurance and in maturity.

Amen.

ঙ

Day 190

HONOR GOD IN ALL THINGS

Whatever I do, I should do all to the glory of God.

(1 Corinthians 10:31)

Whatever I do, whether in word or in deed,
I will do all in the name of the Lord Jesus,
giving thanks to God the Father through Him.

(Colossians 3:17)

Father,

I want to dedicate all that I do this very day to Your glory and honor. There is no component of life that cannot be lived for You, no task so small and mundane that it is unworthy of being offered to Your service. Whether in my speech or in my actions, I will do all in the name of the Lord Jesus, giving thanks through Him to You.

Amen.

Day 191

WALK IN LOVE

I will not let love and truth leave me;
I will bind them around my neck
and write them on the tablet of my heart.

(Proverbs 3:3)

Love is patient, love is kind, it does not envy;
love does not boast, it is not arrogant,
it does not behave rudely; it does not seek its own,
it is not provoked, it keeps no record of wrongs;
it does not rejoice in unrighteousness but
rejoices with the truth;
it bears all things, believes all things,
hopes all things, endures all things.
Love never fails.

(1 Corinthians 13:4-8)

Lord,

The divine love of agape is beyond my power of attainment—it is too high, too deep, too great, because it is a supernatural love that can only come from You. Because the life of Jesus dwells in me, I can walk in the power of His agape and make it evident in the tasks and challenges of daily life.

Amen.

— 🙰 —

Day 192

FOLLOW THE LORD, NOT THE CROWD

I will not follow the crowd in doing wrong.

(Exodus 23:2)

There are six things the Lord hates,
seven that are detestable to Him:
haughty eyes,
a lying tongue,
hands that shed innocent blood,
a heart that devises wicked plans,
feet that run swiftly to evil,
a false witness who breathes lies,
and one who causes strife among brothers.

(Proverbs 6:16-19)

Lord,

I wish to be pleasing to You, and I desire a growth in the holy fear of displeasing You through indulgence in the things You have revealed that You hate. Keep me far from pride, deception, bloodguilt, wickedness, evil actions, slander, and strife—and draw me to the beauty and innocence of holiness.

Amen.

Day 193

BEWARE OF ALL FORMS OF PRIDE

When I am blessed with abundance,
I will beware lest my heart becomes proud,
and I forget the Lord my God who provided all good
things, thinking that it was my power and the strength
of my hand that brought this wealth.

(Deuteronomy 8:12-14, 17)

Pride goes before destruction,
and a haughty spirit before a fall.

(Proverbs 16:18)

Lord God,

May I ever cultivate the wisdom of gratitude in all things so that I remember that every good thing comes from Your hand. You graciously provide me with far more than I deserve, and I acknowledge that it is Your power and the strength of Your hand that has blessed me.

Amen.

&

Day 194

BE STRONG IN THE LORD

I will be strong and courageous;
I will not be afraid or discouraged because
of my adversaries,
for there is a greater power with me than with them,
for the Lord my God is with me to help me.

(2 Chronicles 32:7-8)

I will not be afraid of my adversaries,
but I will remember the Lord, who is
great and awesome.

(Nehemiah 4:14)

Dear Lord,

Since my confidence is wholly in You, I will stand firm and not be dismayed at the adversities which come into my path. I know that I am more than a conqueror in Christ Jesus and that I am an overcomer in the spiritual warfare as I abide in Him.

Amen.

Day 195

SERVE GOD OUT OF A WILLING HEART

The Lord my God wants me to fear Him,
to walk in all His ways, to love Him,
and to serve the Lord my God
with all my heart and with all my soul.

(Deuteronomy 10:12)

I want to know God and serve Him
with a whole heart and with a willing mind;
for the Lord searches all hearts
and understands every motive behind the thoughts.

(1 Chronicles 28:9)

O Lord my God,

May I fear You, walk in all Your ways, love You and serve You with all my heart and with all my soul. I ask for a whole heart and a willing mind so that I will please You in my thoughts, in my words, and in my actions.

Amen.

Day 196

UNDERSTAND GOD'S PURPOSE FOR DISCIPLINE

I will endure discipline, for God is treating me as a son.
For what son is not disciplined by his father?
If I am without discipline, of which all have become
partakers, then I am an illegitimate child and not a true
son. Moreover, we have all had human fathers who
disciplined us, and we respected them; how much more
should I be subjected to the Father of spirits and live?

(Hebrews 12:7-9)

Our fathers disciplined us for a little while as they
thought best, but God disciplines us for our good,
that we may share in His holiness.
No discipline seems pleasant at the time, but painful;
later on, however, it produces the peaceable fruit of
righteousness for those who have been trained by it.

(Hebrews 12:10-11)

Heavenly Father,

I know that through the redemption which is in Christ
Jesus, I have been born again into Your family. Since I
am Your child, You love me and discipline me for my
good. The process may be painful, but the outcome of this
training is the peaceable fruit of righteousness. I subject
myself to You, the Father of spirits.

Amen.

Day 197

WELCOME INSTRUCTION AND CORRECTION

Instruct a wise man, and he will be wiser still;
teach a righteous man, and he will increase in learning.

(Proverbs 9:9)

He who heeds instruction is on the path of life,
but he who refuses correction goes astray.

(Proverbs 10:17)

Lord,

I pray for the wisdom to heed and treasure instruction in
the path of life. Without Your training and correction, I
will go astray and miss the purpose for which I was called.
May I listen to your teaching and value Your instruction
by putting it into practice.

Amen.

~~~

Day 198

HOLD FAST TO GOD IN AFFLICTION

Before I was afflicted I went astray,
but now I keep Your word.

It was good for me to be afflicted,
so that I might learn Your statutes.

(Psalm 119:67, 71)

I will not forget the exhortation that
addresses me as a son:
"My son, do not despise the Lord's discipline,
nor lose heart when you are rebuked by Him,
for those whom the Lord loves He disciplines,
and He chastises every son whom He receives."

(Hebrews 12:5-6)

Father,

The discipline and chastisement that comes from Your
loving hand is always for my highest good. Because
of Your sovereign care, rebukes and afflictions actually
lead to clarity and understanding so that I will be refined
and purified for Your purposes. I therefore submit to Your
exhortation, Your timing, and Your intentions.

Amen.

Day 199

PUT YOUR PRIDE IN THE LORD

The fear of the Lord is the instruction for wisdom,
and humility comes before honor.

(Proverbs 15:33)

Thus says the Lord:
"Let not the wise man boast of his wisdom, and let not
the strong man boast of his strength, and let not the rich
man boast of his riches; but let him who boasts boast
about this: that he understands and knows Me,
that I am the Lord, who exercises lovingkindness, justice,
and righteousness on earth; for in these I delight,"
declares the Lord.

(Jeremiah 9:23-24)

Dear Lord,

Grant me the grace to order my steps in the path of
humility and the fear of the Lord. I will not boast in
the things that are so impressive to people—shrewdness,
power, and wealth—but in the knowledge of You.
Since You delight in lovingkindness, justice, and
righteousness, I want to treasure these above whatever the
world has to offer.

Amen.

∞

Day 200

BE SLOW TO ANGER

He who is slow to anger is better than the mighty,
and he who rules his spirit than he who takes a city.

(Proverbs 16:32)

In my anger I will not sin;
I will not let the sun go down while I am still angry,
and I will not give the devil a foothold.

(Ephesians 4:26-27)

Heavenly Father,

May I have the wisdom and skill to restrain myself and practice self-control during the times when my patience is tested and my desires are thwarted. May I practice graceful discipline and disciplined grace as I seek to respond to unpredictable circumstances with calmness, poise, grace, and peace.

Amen.

Day 201

PURSUE RIGHTEOUSNESS AND LOVE

He who pursues righteousness and love
finds life, righteousness, and honor.

(Proverbs 21:21)

The goal of our instruction is love,
which comes from a pure heart
and a good conscience and a sincere faith.

(1 Timothy 1:5)

Lord,

Grant that I would grow to desire Your presence, righteousness, and love more than all earthly blessings and benefits. Knowing that I am beloved of You, may I love others by putting their needs above my own. Through the indwelling power of your Holy Spirit, I ask for a pure heart, a good conscience, and a sincere faith.

Amen.

Day 202

MEDITATE ON THE WORD

I will not let Your word depart from my mouth,
but I will meditate on it day and night,
so that I may be careful to do according to all that
is written in it; for then I will make my way
prosperous, and I will act wisely.

(Joshua 1:8)

I am committed to God and to the word of His grace,
which is able to build me up and give me an inheritance
among all those who are sanctified.

(Acts 20:32)

Dear God,

I ask for the wisdom to establish all that I think, say, and do upon the foundation of your timeless word. May I be increasingly rooted in the truths of Your revelation and grow in my commitment to be a doer and not merely a hearer of Your wisdom. Sanctify me by Your word—Your word is truth.

Amen.

Truth

Introduction to Truth

Since God is the unchanging wellspring of the true, the good, and the beautiful, truth is what God says about a thing. We live in a culture that seeks to reduce truth to subjective experience and opinion, but the countercultural message of Scripture is that there is an objective source of truth in the personal revelation of the living God through the prophets, the apostles, and most decisively, in the incarnate Word, the living logos who became one of us (Hebrews 1:1-4).

The Bible is rich in narrative and story, and these stories are conveyors of truth, insight, and understanding. Because of this, I have decided to convey biblical truths in this book by making a truth statement, following it with Scripture, and illustrating it with a brief story or narrative.

Day 203

GOD HAS A PURPOSE FOR OUR LIVES

For even the Son of Man did not come to be served,
but to serve, and to give His life a ransom for many.

(Mark 10:45)

For the Son of Man has come to seek
and to save that which was lost.

(Luke 19:10)

I glorified You on the earth, having accomplished the
work which You have given Me to do.

(John 17:4)

In 1902 Meyer Kubelski, a Jewish immigrant from Russia, gave his son a violin for his eighth birthday. It cost Meyer $50, a small fortune in those days.

The son loved music and soon was playing well enough to give concerts at the Barrison Theater in Waukeegan, the town where the Kubelskis lived. By the age of 18 he had teamed up with a woman pianist as a concert team in vaudeville.

One night as Benjamin Kubelski was playing, he felt impelled, between numbers, to tell the audience about a funny incident that had happened to him during the day. "The audience laughed," he recalled later, "and the sound intoxicated me. That laughter ended my days as a musician." Jack Benny, as the young Kubelski later called himself, had found his rightful career.

What is God's purpose for your life? Ask God to give you a clear sense of purpose that combines ability with passion.

Day 204

WE ARE CALLED TO LOVE AND SERVE PEOPLE

God raised me up with Christ and seated me with Him
in the heavenly realms in Christ Jesus,
in order that in the coming ages
He might show the surpassing riches of His grace
in kindness toward me in Christ Jesus.

(Ephesians 2:6-7)

The fruit of the Spirit is love, joy, peace,
patience, kindness, goodness,
faithfulness, gentleness, self-control;
against such things there is no law.

(Galatians 5:22-23)

⁓

Sir William Osler, visiting one of London's leading children's hospitals, noticed that in a convalescent ward all the children were clustered at one end of the room dressing their dolls, playing games, and playing in the sandbox—all except for one little girl, who sat forlornly on the edge of her high, narrow bed, clutching a cheap doll.

The great physician looked at the lonely little figure, then at the ward nurse. "We've tried to get Susan to play," the nurse whispered, "but the other children just won't have anything to do with her. You see, no one comes to see her. Her mother is dead, and her father has been here just once—he brought her that doll. The children have a strange code. Visitors mean so much. If you don't have any visitors, you are ignored."

Sir William walked over to the child's bed and asked in a voice loud enough for the others to hear, "May I sit down, please?" The little girl's eyes lit up. "I can't stay very long this visit," Osler went on, "but I have wanted to see you so badly."

For five minutes he sat talking with her, even inquiring about her doll's health and solemnly pulling out his stethoscope to listen to the doll's chest. And as he left, he turned to the youngster and said in a carrying voice, "You won't forget our secret, will you? And mind, don't tell anyone."

At the door he looked back. His new friend was now the center of a curious and admiring throng.

A small act of kindness, a word of encouragement, a deed of grace in the life of another can make a lasting difference.

Day 205

OUR NEW IDENTITY IN CHRIST MAKES US SECURE

Blessed be the God and Father
of our Lord Jesus Christ,
who has blessed us with every spiritual blessing
in the heavenly realms in Christ.

(Ephesians 1:3)

If anyone is in Christ, he is a new creation; the old things
passed away; behold, they have become new.

(2 Corinthians 5:17)

—————————————— ଓ ——————————————

Joe Louis was the world heavyweight boxing champion from 1937 until he retired in 1949. During his time of service in the army, Louis was driving with a fellow GI when he was involved in a minor collision with a large truck. The truck driver got out, yelling and swearing at Louis, who just sat in the driver's seat, smiling. "Why didn't you get out and knock him flat?" asked his buddy after the truck driver had moved on. "Why should I?" replied Joe. "When somebody insulted Caruso, did he sing an aria for him?"

This story well illustrates the theme of identity. The truck driver clearly didn't know the real identity of the person he was cursing, for if he had, he would have treated him in a dramatically different way! On the other hand, Joe Louis knew who he was—the best boxer in the world—and therefore he had nothing to prove. Many other men in his position would have been tempted to fight back or at least return insult for insult. But Louis was secure enough in his identity to understand that such a response would only be degrading. The truck driver's opinion of him was irrelevant to Joe's self-understanding.

Day 206

ETERNAL DESTINIES
ARE AT STAKE

God so loved the world that He gave His only begotten
Son, that whoever believes in Him
should not perish but have eternal life.
For God did not send His Son into the world
to condemn the world,
but to save the world through Him.

(John 3:16-17)

The harvest is plentiful, but the workers are few.
Therefore, ask the Lord of the harvest
to send out workers into His harvest.

(Matthew 9:37-38; Luke 10:2)

I like to tell the tale of the airplane that had four people and only three parachutes. There was the pilot, a genius, a minister, and a Boy Scout. When the engine caught fire and the plane began to go down, the pilot ran out, grabbed one of the parachutes, and bailed out. The genius stood up and said, "I am the world's smartest man! The world needs what I have to offer." He grabbed one and jumped out, leaving the minister and the scout. The minister told the boy, "Your whole life is before you — take the last parachute." The scout answered, "Don't sweat it, mister — the world's smartest man just bailed out with my backpack!" In a very real sense, the world is going down in flames, and people are putting their hope in the backpacks of works, merit, possessions, position, and power. But the gospel tells that the only true parachute is Jesus Christ.

We need to remember what is at stake. "He who has the Son has the life; he who does not have the Son of God does not have the life" (1 John 5:12). The stakes associated with the message we share are high, for they involve nothing less than people's eternal destiny.

Day 207

REMEMBERING THE THINGS THAT REALLY MATTER

Let us consider how to stir up one another
toward love and good works,
not forsaking our own meeting together,
as some are in the habit of doing,
but encouraging one another,
and all the more as we see the day approaching.

(Hebrews 10:24-25)

Seek first His kingdom and His righteousness,
and all these things will be added to you.

(Matthew 6:33; Luke 12:31)

Listen to Thomas Boswell's observations on our age in his book, *Why Time Begins on Opening Day:*

"**B**orn to an age where horror has become commonplace, where tragedy has, by its monotonous repetition, become a parody of sorrow, we need to fence off a few parks where humans try to be fair, where skill has some hope of reward, where absurdity has a harder time than usual getting a ticket."

The distorted values, images, and icons of our culture flow out of a growing tendency to view truth, goodness, and beauty as subjective and relative, not objective and absolute. All the rules change when we replace accountability to God with the autonomous self. In such a time as this, we desperately need the refuge, nurture, and sanity of the "parks" of corporate life in Christ. When members of the body of Christ gather together for worship, edification, and fellowship, they remind one another of the things that really matter and encourage one another to "seek first His kingdom and His righteousness" (Matthew 6:33).

Day 208

QUIETING THE RESTLESS HEART

Be anxious for nothing, but in everything by prayer
and petition with thanksgiving, let your requests
be known to God. And the peace of God,
which transcends all understanding,
will guard your hearts and minds in Christ Jesus.

(Philippians 4:6-7)

I have learned to be content in whatever
circumstances I am.
Whether I am abased or in abundance,
whether I am filled or hungry,
I have learned the secret of being content in any and
every situation.
I can do all things through Him who strengthens me.

(Philippians 4:11-13)

In The Image: A Guide to Pseudo-Events in America, author Daniel Boorstin comments on the inconsistent and extravagant expectations of contemporary Americans:

"We expect anything and everything. We expect the contradictory and the impossible. We expect compact cars which are spacious; luxurious cars which are economical. We expect to be rich and charitable, powerful and merciful, active and reflective, kind and competitive. . . . We expect to eat and stay thin, to be constantly on the move and ever more neighborly, to go to a 'church of our choice' and yet feel its guiding power over us, to revere God and to be God. Never have people been more the masters of their environment. Yet never has a people expected so much more than the world could offer."

Many of us enjoy more luxuries and options than kings in earlier times could have conceived. Yet our trinkets and toys, gadgets and gewgaws have not satisfied us, but have left us more restless than ever. This should come as no surprise to followers of Jesus who have come to understand Augustine's words: "You have made us for Yourself, O Lord, and our hearts are restless until they rest in You."

Day 209

THE SECRET OF CONTENTMENT

I will keep my life free from the love of money
and be content with what I have,
for You have said,
"I will never leave you, nor will I forsake you."

(Hebrews 13:5)

I will not love the world or the things in the world.
If anyone loves the world, the love of the Father
is not in him.
For all that is in the world — the lust of the flesh,
the lust of the eyes, and the pride of life —
is not of the Father but of the world.
And the world and its lusts are passing away,
but the one who does the will of God abides forever.

(1 John 2:15-17)

&

"We want a whole race perpetually in pursuit of the rainbow's end, never honest, nor kind, nor happy now, but always using as mere fuel wherewith to heap the altar of the future every real gift which is offered them in the Present." Uncle Screwtape's diabolical counsel to his nephew Wormwood in C. S. Lewis' *The Screwtape Letters* is a reminder that most of us live more in the future than in the present. Somehow we think that the days ahead will make up for what we perceive to be our present lack. We think, "When I get this or when that happens, then I'll be happy," but this is an exercise in self-deception that overlooks the fact that even when we get what we want, it never delivers what it promised.

Most of us don't know precisely what we want, but we are certain we don't have it. Driven by dissatisfaction, we pursue the treasure at the end of the rainbow and rarely drink deeply at the well of the present moment, which is all we ever have. The truth is that if we are not satisfied with what we have, we will never be satisfied with what we want.

Day 210

THE DISCIPLINE OF GRATITUDE

I will give thanks to the Lord, call upon His name,
and make known to others what He has done.
I will sing to Him, sing praises to Him,
and tell of all His wonderful acts.

(1 Chronicles 16:8-9)

I will rejoice always, pray without ceasing,
and give thanks in all circumstances,
for this is God's will for me in Christ Jesus.

(1 Thessalonians 5:16-18)

⟡

A young man with a bandaged hand approached the clerk at the post office. "Sir, could you please address this post card for me?" The clerk did so gladly, and then agreed to write a message on the card.

He then asked, "Is there anything else I can do for you?" The young man looked at the card for a moment and then said, "Yes, add a PS: 'Please excuse the handwriting.'"

We are an ungrateful people. Writing of man in Notes from the Underground, Dostoevsky says, "If he is not stupid, he is monstrously ungrateful! Phenomenally ungrateful. In fact, I believe that the best definition of man is the ungrateful biped." Luke's account of the cleansing of the ten lepers underscores the human tendency to expect grace as our due and to forget to thank God for His benefits. "Were there not ten cleansed? But the nine— where are they? Was no one found who turned back to give glory to God, except this foreigner?" (Luke 17:17-18).

Day 211

TIME IS OUR MOST PRECIOUS ASSET

Lord, make me to know my end
and what is the measure of my days;
let me know how fleeting is my life.

(Psalm 39:4)

Teach me to number my days,
that I may gain a heart of wisdom.

(Psalm 90:12)

℠

Suppose your doctor tells you, after a routine physical examination, that you have a terminal illness. You seek a second and third opinion, and all agree that at best you have one year to live. There will be no discernible effects of the disease until it has reached its course.

How would this scenario affect your vision of life, your roles on this earth, and the way you should invest your remaining time? The degree to which it would alter your present perspective and practice is the distance between your current view of life and the biblical view of life. The latter emphasizes the brevity of our earthly sojourn and stresses the urgency of investing our most precious asset, time, in a way that will have lasting consequences. The former view typically denies the imminence of death and, for all practical purposes, treats the temporal as though it were eternal.

Day 212

THE FEAR OF THE LORD

Great is the Lord and most worthy of praise;
He is to be feared above all gods.
For all the gods of the nations are idols,
but the Lord made the heavens.
Splendor and majesty are before Him;
strength and beauty are in His sanctuary.
I will ascribe to the Lord glory and strength.
I will ascribe to the Lord the glory due His name
and worship the Lord in the beauty of holiness.

(Psalm 96:4-8)

Who is the man that fears the Lord?
He will instruct him in the way he should choose.

(Psalm 25:12)

━━━━━━━━━━━━━━━ ☙ ━━━━━━━━━━━━━━━

We would be wise to cultivate a holy fear, awe, and wonder before the magnificence, might, glory, and greatness of the Creator and Ruler of heaven and earth. Like John, when we see the glorified Christ, what we now dimly perceive about His powers and perfections will become much more clear. Perhaps we will react as did two of the animals in *The Wind in the Willows* when they saw "the Piper at the Gate of Dawn":

"Rat!" he found breath to whisper, shaking. "Are you afraid?"

"Afraid?" murmured the Rat, his eyes shining with unutterable love. "Afraid! Of Him? O, never, never! And yet—and yet—O Mole, I am afraid!"

Then the two animals, crouching to the earth, bowed their heads and did worship.

"The fear of the Lord is the beginning of wisdom,
and the knowledge of the Holy One
is understanding"

(Proverbs 9:10).

Day 213

THE GRAIN OF YOUR CHARACTER

I am hard pressed on every side, but not crushed;
perplexed, but not in despair;
persecuted, but not forsaken;
struck down, but not destroyed;
always carrying about in my body the death of Jesus,
so that the life of Jesus may also be revealed in my body.
For we who live are always being delivered over to
death for Jesus' sake,
so that His life may be revealed in our mortal body.

(2 Corinthians 4:8-11)

I will fight the good fight of faith
and lay hold of the eternal life to which I was called
when I made the good confession in the presence
of many witnesses.
In the sight of God, who gives life to all things,
and of Christ Jesus, who testified the good confession
before Pontius Pilate,
I want to keep this command without blemish
or reproach
until the appearing of our Lord Jesus Christ,
which God will bring about in His own time.

(1 Timothy 6:12-15a)

တ

There is a story about a traveler in a logging area who watched with curiosity as a lumberjack occasionally jabbed his sharp hook into a log to separate it from the others floating down a mountain stream. When asked why he did this, the logger replied, "These may all look alike to you, but I can recognize that a few of them are quite different. The ones I let pass are from trees that grew in a valley where they were always protected from the storms. Their grain is rather coarse. The ones I have hooked and kept apart came from high on the mountains. From the time they were small they were beaten by strong winds. This toughens the trees and gives them a fine grain. We save them for choice work. They are too good to be used for ordinary lumber."

The grain of your character is being finely arranged by the toughening action of life's trials and adversities. "Before I was afflicted I went astray, but now I keep Your word" (Psalm 119:67, cf. vv. 71, 75).

Day 214

GOD MADE US FOR A PURPOSE

Having the firstfruits of the Spirit,
I groan inwardly as I wait eagerly for my adoption,
the redemption of my body.
For in hope I have been saved,
but hope that is seen is not hope;
for who hopes for what he sees?
But if I hope for what I do not yet see,
I eagerly wait for it with perseverance.

(Romans 8:23-25)

I have not been made perfect, but I press on
to lay hold of that for which Christ Jesus also
laid hold of me.
I do not consider myself yet to have attained it,
but one thing I do: forgetting what is behind
and stretching forward to what is ahead,
I press on toward the goal to win the prize
of the upward call of God in Christ Jesus.

(Philippians 3:12-14)

In the film *Chariots of Fire*, there is a significant scene when Eric Liddell takes his sister Jennie for a walk in the hills of Scotland to explain his commitment to training for the 1924 Olympic Games in Paris. He tells her, "I've decided—I'm going back to China. The missionary service accepted me." Jennie rejoices to hear this, since she fears her brother's calling to be a missionary is being threatened by his interest in running.

However, Eric goes on to say, "But I've got a lot of running to do first. Jennie—Jennie, you've got to understand. I believe that God made me for a purpose—for China. But He also made me fast! And when I run, I feel His pleasure. To give it up would be to hold Him in contempt. You were right. It's not just fun. To win is to honor Him."

Liddell was a man of focus and passion because he pursued a growing sense of God's purpose for his life. "When I run, I feel His pleasure"—what do you do that makes you feel God's pleasure? Frederick Buechner put it this way in *Wishful Thinking: A Theological ABC*: "The place God calls you to is the place where your deep gladness and the world's deep hunger meet." As you become a person of calling and purpose, you come to realize that God's good pleasure is also your good pleasure. Seek satisfaction apart from Him, and you will never find it; seek to please Him first, and you discover that satisfaction is a byproduct of the pursuit of God.

Day 215

GRATITUDE IS A CHOICE

Bless the Lord, O my soul,
and forget not all His benefits;
who forgives all your iniquities and
heals all your diseases;
who redeems your life from the pit
and crowns you with love and compassion;
who satisfies your desires with good things,
so that your youth is renewed like the eagle's.

(Psalm 103:2-5)

We should not get drunk on wine,
for that is dissipation.
Instead, we should be filled with the Spirit,
speaking to one another with psalms, hymns,
and spiritual songs;
singing and making music in our hearts to the Lord,
always giving thanks to God the Father for everything,
in the name of our Lord Jesus Christ.

(Ephesians 5:18-20)

Gratitude is a choice, not merely a feeling, and it requires effort especially in difficult times. But the more we choose to live in the discipline of conscious thanksgiving, the more natural it becomes, and the more our eyes are opened to the little things throughout the course of the day that we previously overlooked. G. K. Chesterton had a way of acknowledging these many little benefits: "You say grace before meals. All right. But I say grace before the concert and the opera, and grace before the play and pantomime, and grace before I open a book, and grace before sketching, painting, swimming, fencing, boxing, walking, playing, dancing and grace before I dip the pen in the ink."

Henri Nouwen observed that "every gift I acknowledge reveals another and another until, finally, even the most normal, obvious, and seemingly mundane event or encounter proves to be filled with grace."

Day 216

ALL TRUTH COMES FROM GOD

In the beginning was the Word,
and the Word was with God,
and the Word was God.
He was in the beginning with God.

(John 1:1-2)

There is but one God, the Father,
from whom all things came and for whom I live;
and there is but one Lord, Jesus Christ,
through whom all things came and
through whom I live.

(1 Corinthians 8:6)

Imagine someone from an illiterate culture who stumbles upon a New Testament left inadvertently by a traveling missionary. The native picks up the strange object and brings it to the elders of his village, but since they have never heard of reading or writing, they are unable to discern the meaning of the mysterious black markings on the pages. They may even come to revere the alien object, but unless an outsider comes and explains it to them, the living words it contains will never be more than dark squiggles on a gossamer white substance.

Our world is like that book; unless an Outsider explains it to us, we will reduce its glory to the impersonal forces of time plus chance, or we will worship the creature rather than the Creator. But this is a failure to grasp the higher levels of meaning—the markings are letters, the letters combine into words, the words conform to grammatical principles and form sentences, the sentences convey ideas, the ideas lead to aesthetic, ethical, and spiritual truth, and all truth comes from the infinite-personal God.

Day 217

THE IMITATION OF CHRIST

Your lovingkindness, O Lord, reaches to the heavens,
Your faithfulness to the skies.
Your righteousness is like the mountains of God;
Your judgments are like a great deep.
O Lord, You preserve man and beast.
How priceless is Your lovingkindness, O God!
The children of men find refuge in the
shadow of Your wings.
For with You is the fountain of life;
in Your light we see light.

(Psalm 36:5-7, 9)

I acknowledge this day and take it to my heart
that the Lord is God in heaven above and
on the earth below;
there is no other.

(Deuteronomy 4:39)

Ⓞ my soul, above all things and in all things always rest in the Lord, for He is the eternal rest of the saints.

Grant me most sweet and loving Jesus, to rest in You above every other creature, above all health and beauty, above all glory and honor, above all power and dignity, above all knowledge and precise thought, above all wealth and talent, above all joy and exultation, above all fame and praise, above all sweetness and consolation, above all hope and promise, above all merit and desire, above all gifts and favors You give and shower upon me, above all happiness and joy that the mind can understand and feel, and finally, above all angels and archangels, above all the hosts of heaven, above all things visible and invisible, and above all that is not You, my God.

—Thomas à Kempis, *The Imitation of Christ*

Day 218

NOTHING LESS THAN GOD WILL SATISFY US

God is my strong fortress, and He sets
the blameless free in His way.
He makes my feet like the feet of a deer;
He enables me to stand on the heights.
He trains my hands for battle, so that my arms
can bend a bow of bronze.
You give me Your shield of victory;
You stoop down to make me great.
You broaden the path beneath me, and
my feet have not slipped.

(2 Samuel 22:33-37)

May the God of peace, who through the blood
of the eternal covenant
brought back from the dead our Lord Jesus,
that great Shepherd of the sheep,
equip me in every good thing to do His will,
working in me what is pleasing in His sight,
through Jesus Christ, to whom be glory forever and ever.

(Hebrews 13:20-21)

Six hundred years ago, Julian of Norwich, in her *Revelations of Divine Love* asked God for the three faithful wounds of contrition for her sins, compassion for others, and an intense longing for God. She wrote, "At the same moment the Trinity filled me full of heartfelt joy, and I knew that all eternity was like this for those who attain heaven. For the Trinity is God, and God the Trinity; the Trinity is our Maker and keeper, our eternal lover, joy and bliss—all through our Lord Jesus Christ. . . . We have got to realize the littleness of creation and to see it for the nothing that it is before we can love and possess God who is uncreated. This is the reason why we have no ease of heart or soul, for we are seeking our rest in trivial things which cannot satisfy, and not seeking to know God, almighty, all-wise, all-good. He is true rest. It is His will that we should know Him, and His pleasure that we should rest in Him. Nothing less will satisfy us. . . . We shall never cease wanting and longing until we possess Him in fullness and joy. Then we shall have no further wants. Meanwhile His will is that we go on knowing and loving until we are perfected in heaven. . . . The more clearly the soul sees the blessed face by grace and love, the more it longs to see it in its fullness."

Day 219

THE BOUNDLESS LOVE OF GOD

Many, O Lord my God, are the wonders You have done,
and Your thoughts toward us no one can recount to You;
were I to speak and tell of them, they would be
too many to declare.

(Psalm 40:5)

I am convinced that neither death nor life,
nor angels nor principalities, nor things present
nor things to come,
nor powers, nor height nor depth, nor
anything else in all creation,
will be able to separate me from the love of God
that is in Christ Jesus my Lord.

(Romans 8:38-39)

The Elizabethan poet George Herbert (1593-1633) captured this stinging sense of unworthiness in his superb personification of the love of God:

Love bade me welcome; yet my soul drew back,
 Conscious of dust and sin.
But quick-eyed Love, observing me grow slack
 From my first entrance in,
Drew nearer to me, sweetly questioning,
 If I lacked anything.
"A guest," I answered, "worthy to be here."
 Love said, "You shall be he."
"I, the unkind, ungrateful? Ah, my dear,
 I cannot look on thee."
Love took my hand, and smiling did reply,
 "Who made the eyes but I?"
"Truth, Lord, but I have marred them; let my shame
 Go where it doth deserve."
"And know you not," says Love, "who bore the blame?"
 "My dear, then I will serve."
"You must sit down," says Love, "and taste my meat."
 So I did sit and eat.

Beyond all human faith, beyond all earthbound hope, the eternal God of love has reached down to us, and in the ultimate act of sacrifice, purchased us and made us His own.

Day 220

IT'S ALL IN YOUR PERSPECTIVE

No one who waits for You will be ashamed,
but those who are treacherous without cause
will be ashamed.
Show me Your ways, O Lord, teach me Your paths;
lead me in Your truth and teach me,
for You are the God of my salvation,
and my hope is in You all day long.

(Psalm 25:3-5)

Now I am a child of God, and what I shall be
has not yet been revealed.
I know that when He is revealed, I shall be like Him, for
I shall see Him as He is.
And everyone who has this hope in Him
purifies himself, just as He is pure.

(1 John 3:2-3)

⌘

An optimist said to a pessimist, "Isn't this a bright, sunny day?" The pessimist replied, "Yes, but if this heat spell doesn't stop soon, all the grass will burn up."

Two days later, the optimist said to the pessimist, "Isn't this rain wonderful?" The pessimist replied, "Well, if it doesn't stop soon, my garden will wash away."

The next day, the optimist invited the pessimist to go duck hunting. The optimist wanted to show off his new registered hunting dog that could do things no other dog could. The pessimist looked at the dog and said, "Looks like a mutt to me."

At that moment, a flock of ducks flew over. The optimist shot one of the ducks and it fell in the middle of the lake. He snapped his fingers and his new dog ran after the duck. The dog ran out on the water, picked up the duck, and ran back on the water. The optimist took the duck from the dog's mouth, turned to the pessimist, and said, "What do you think of my dog now?" The pessimist replied, "Dumb dog—can't even swim!"

An eternal perspective enables us to see clearly; a temporal perspective clouds the truth.

Day 221

TEACH US TO NUMBER OUR DAYS

I will guard my heart with all diligence,
for out of it flow the issues of life.

(Proverbs 4:23)

We have the prophetic word made more certain,
to which we will do well to pay attention,
as to a light shining in a dark place,
until the day dawns and the morning star
rises in our hearts.

(2 Peter 1:19)

∽

"Because we do not know when we will die, we get to think of life as an inexhaustible well. And yet everything happens only a certain number of times. And a very small number, really. How many times will you remember a certain afternoon of your childhood, an afternoon that is so deeply a part of your being that you can't even conceive of your life without it? Perhaps four or five times more? Perhaps not even that. How many more times will you watch the full moon rise? Perhaps twenty. And yet it all seems limitless."

Actor Brandon Lee made these poignant observations in his last interview before his death in 1993 after completing the film, *The Crow*. Who would have known that he would be ushered into eternity so soon after his comments on the brevity of life? Lee was right to say that we cannot presume on the future, even though most people do just that by assuming that their lives are limitless.

As Moses prayed near the end of his life, "So teach us to number our days, that we may present to You a heart of wisdom" (Psalm 90:12).

Day 222

ONLY TWO DAYS ON OUR CALENDAR

I know that my Redeemer lives
and that in the end He will stand upon the earth.
And after my skin has been destroyed,
yet in my flesh I will see God;
whom I myself will see and behold with my own eyes
and not another.
How my heart yearns within me!

(Job 19:25-27)

I will judge nothing before the time,
until the Lord comes,
who will bring to light what is hidden in darkness
and will expose the motives of men's hearts;
and then each one's praise will come from God.

(1 Corinthians 4:5)

Only two things on earth will go into eternity — God's Word and people. God has placed us here to grow in Christ and to reproduce the life of Christ in others. Each of us has specific opportunities to do this in our own spheres of influence, and as we abide in Christ and let His words abide in us, we will bear lasting fruit (John 15:7-8), and the living God will confirm the work of our hands.

The great saints along the way learned the wisdom of having only two days on their calendars: "today" and "that day" (the day they would be with the Lord). If we want a heart of wisdom, we should learn to live each today in light of that day. When we daily remind ourselves of the real purpose for our sojourn on earth, we will cultivate an eternal perspective that influences all our work and all our relationships. In 2 Corinthians 4:16-18, Paul summarized the vision that determined the course of his life:

"Therefore we do not lose heart, but though our outer man is decaying, yet our inner man is being renewed day by day. For momentary, light affliction is producing for us an eternal weight of glory far beyond all comparison, while we look not at the things which are seen, but at the things which are not seen; for the things which are seen are temporal, but the things which are not seen are eternal."

Day 223

CHANCE VERSUS DESIGN

Since the creation of the world God's invisible
attributes—His eternal power and divine nature—
have been clearly seen,
being understood from what has been made,
so that men are without excuse.

(Romans 1:20)

The heavens declare the glory of God,
and the skies proclaim the work of His hands.
Day after day they pour forth speech;
night after night they reveal knowledge.

(Psalm 19:1-2)

∞

In *The God Who Is There*, Francis Schaeffer refers to the American composer John Cage who believes that the universe is impersonal by nature and that it originated only through pure chance. In an attempt to live consistently with this personal philosophy, Cage composes all of his music by various chance agencies. He uses, among other things, the tossing of coins and the rolling of dice to make sure that no personal element enters into the final product. The result is music that has no form, no structure and, for the most part, no appeal. Though Cage's professional life accurately reflects his belief in a universe that has no order, his personal life does not, for his favorite pastime is mycology, the collecting of mushrooms, and because of the potentially lethal results of picking a wrong mushroom, he cannot approach it on a purely by-chance basis. Concerning that, he states: "I became aware that if I approached mushrooms in the spirit of my chance operations, I would die shortly." John Cage "believes" one thing, but practices another. In doing so, he is an example of the person described in Romans 1:18 who "suppresses the truth of God," for when faced with the certainty of order in the universe, he still clings to his theory of randomness.

Day 224

THE YEARNING FOR A FINAL RETURN

The Lord God will swallow up death forever,
and He will wipe away the tears from all faces; He will
remove the reproach of His people from all the earth.
For the Lord has spoken.
And it will be said in that day, "Behold, this is our God;
we have waited for Him, and He will save us.
This is the Lord, we have trusted in Him;
let us rejoice and be glad in His salvation."

(Isaiah 25:8-9)

The Lord Jesus is coming quickly.
His reward is with Him,
and He will give to everyone according to
what he has done.
He is the Alpha and the Omega,
the First and the Last, the Beginning and the End.
Yes, He is coming quickly.
Amen. Come, Lord Jesus.

(Revelation 22:12-13, 20)

&

Henri Nouwen in his perceptive book, *The Return of the Prodigal Son*, describes his encounter with Rembrandt's painting of this parable and the remarkable effect this painting had on his self-understanding. "It had brought me into touch with something within me that lies far beyond the ups and downs of a busy life, something that represents the ongoing yearning of the human spirit, the yearning for a final return, an unambiguous sense of safety, a lasting home." It is an aspiration to turn to our Father's house and to find the deep satisfaction of His embrace and of being treasured by Him. "In My Father's house are many dwelling places; if it were not so, I would have told you; for I go and prepare a place for you. And if I go and prepare a place for you, I will come again, and receive you to Myself; that where I am, there you may be also" (John 14:2-3).

ॐ

Day 225

THE WAY WE SEE MAKES ALL THE DIFFERENCE

All of us who were baptized into Christ Jesus
were baptized into His death.
I was therefore buried with Him through
baptism into death,
in order that just as Christ was raised from the dead
through the glory of the Father,
so I too may walk in newness of life.

(Romans 6:3-4)

How great is the love the Father has lavished on me,
that I should be called a child of God — and I am!
Therefore the world does not know me,
because it did not know Him.

(1 John 3:1)

∽

In his essay, "Meditation in a Toolshed", C. S. Lewis depicted the difference between looking at a beam of light and looking along the beam. As he entered a dark toolshed, he could see nothing but a sunbeam that came from a crack at the top of the door. At first, he looked at the shaft of light with thousands of specks of dust floating in it, but then he did something most of us have done at one time or another. He moved until the beam fell on his eyes, and at that moment, the toolshed and the sunbeam vanished. Looking along the beam, he saw green leaves moving on the branches of a tree outside, and beyond that, the sun itself. Perspective makes all the difference.

Day 226

THE MUSIC WILL NEVER END

I desire that the God of peace Himself will
sanctify me completely,
and that my whole spirit, soul, and body
will be preserved blameless at the coming of
my Lord Jesus Christ.
He who calls me is faithful, who also will do it.

(1 Thessalonians 5:23-24)

By God's grace I want to live to the end in faith,
knowing that I will not receive the promises on earth,
but seeing them and welcoming them from a distance,
I confess that I am a stranger and a pilgrim on the earth.
Instead, I long for a better country, a heavenly one.
In this way, God will not be ashamed to
be called my God,
for He has prepared a city for me.
Like Moses, I esteem reproach for the sake of Christ
as of greater value than the treasures of this world,
because I am looking to the reward.

(Hebrews 11:13, 16, 26)

Reflection

I used to think—
Loving life so greatly—
That to die would be
Like leaving a party
Before the end.

Now I know that the party
Is really happening
Somewhere else;
That the light and the music—
Escaping in snatches
To make the pulse beat
And the tempo quicken—
Come from a long way
Away.

And I know too
That when I get there
The music will never
End.

—Evangeline Paterson

The saying that "all good things must come to an end" may be true on this earth, but it will not be true of heaven. The sadness of sickness, aging, and death will be swallowed up by our boundless resurrected life in the presence of our Lord and of His people. "Thanks be to God who gives us the victory through our Lord Jesus Christ. Therefore, my beloved brethren, be steadfast, immovable, always abounding in the work of the Lord, knowing that your toil is not in vain in the Lord" (1 Corinthians 15:57-58).

Day 227

OUR RESPONSE TO GOD'S OFFER

"Come now, let us reason together," says the Lord.
"Though your sins are like scarlet,
they shall be as white as snow;
though they are red as crimson,
they shall be like wool."

(Isaiah 1:18)

Unless one is born again, he cannot see
the kingdom of God;
unless one is born of water and the Spirit,
he cannot enter into the kingdom of God.
That which is born of the flesh is flesh,
and that which is born of the Spirit is spirit.
The wind blows wherever it pleases,
and we hear its sound,
but we cannot tell where it comes from,
or where it is going.
So it is with everyone born of the Spirit.

(John 3:3, 5-6, 8)

In 1938, a German merchant vessel was in the midst of a storm in the North Atlantic. The pressure of the sea was so great that the plates in the hull began to buckle, and within moments, the ship sank. Almost miraculously, one sailor stayed afloat by holding onto a cot mattress which had somehow not soaked through and was somewhat buoyant. Then from the south came a British cutter. The German sailor was spotted along with the wreckage of the sunken ship. The British ship "hove to," even though this was a very dangerous thing to do in a storm. The German sailor rose and fell on the billowing waves. A seaman on deck threw out a lifesaver. The big doughnut landed next to the German sailor, but the sailor looked up and saw the British flag and the British faces. He knew that these people represented the traditional enemy of Germany. He turned his back on the lifesaver and slowly the mattress that buoyed him up sank under the waves. The sailor was lost.

When I read this account, I saw it as a parable of God's offer of salvation. Jesus' gift of deliverance from spiritual death is the lifesaver, and part of us instinctively resists taking hold of it because, without Christ, we are enemies of God (Romans 5:10). Like the German sailor, we can stubbornly refuse God's offer, but if we do, we can never blame Him for our demise.

Day 228

CONFORMING TO THE TRUTH

If anyone wishes to come after You,
he must deny himself and take up his cross
and follow You.
For whoever wants to save his life will lose it,
but whoever loses his life for Your sake
and the gospel's will find it.
For what is a man profited if he gains the whole world,
yet forfeits his soul?
Or what will a man give in exchange for his soul?

(Matthew 16:24-26;
Mark 8:34-37;
Luke 9:23-25)

As an obedient child, I will not conform myself
to the former lusts I had when I lived in ignorance,
but as He who called me is holy,
so I will be holy in all my conduct,
because it is written:
"You shall be holy, for I am holy."

(1 Peter 1:14-16)

The prominent nineteenth-century British actor William Charles Macready (1793-1873) was noted for his tragic roles, but his handwriting was notoriously difficult to decipher. When he wrote a complimentary letter of admission to a theater during one of his American tours, the recipient remarked that it looked every bit as illegible as a doctor's prescription. He and a friend thereupon decided to take it along to the apothecary to see what he made of it. The young assistant took the piece of paper and with scarcely a glance at it began pulling down phials and jars to make a compound. After mixing a number of ingredients with great confidence, he seemed to come to an item that bothered him; he paused and puzzled over it and at last summoned his boss from the back of the shop. The older man studied the paper and then with a contemptuous snort at his assistant's ignorance, pulled down another bottle and completed the mixture. Handing the result to his customers, he remarked with a smile, "A cough mixture, and a very good one. Fifty cents, if you please."

We have a way of interpreting things according to our expectations, rather than altering our preconceptions to conform to the truth.

Day 229

EMBRACING AN ETERNAL PERSPECTIVE

I wait for the Lord;
my soul waits, and in His word I put my hope.
I hope in the Lord,
for with Him is unfailing love and abundant
redemption.

(Psalm 130:5, 7)

I have hope in God,
that there will be a resurrection of both
the righteous and the wicked.
In view of this,
I strive always to keep my conscience
blameless before God and men.

(Acts 24:15-16)

Years ago, a minister waited in line to have his car filled with gas just before a long holiday weekend. The attendant worked quickly, but there were many cars ahead of him in front of the service station. Finally, the attendant motioned him toward a vacant pump.

"Reverend," said the young man, "sorry about the delay. It seems as if everyone waits until the last minute to get ready for a long trip." The minister chuckled, "I know what you mean. It's the same in my business."

If ours is an eternal perspective, we will gripped by the biblical truth that our brief earthly sojourn is designed to prepare us for an eternal heavenly citizenship. The more we align ourselves with this perspective, the more it will have an impact on our short-term and long-term priorities.

Day 230

THE CRIME OF A WASTED LIFE

Behold, the Lord God will come with power,
and His arm will rule for Him.
Behold, His reward is with Him,
and His recompense accompanies Him.
He will feed His flock like a shepherd;
He will gather the lambs in His arms
and carry them close to His heart;
He will gently lead those that have young.

(Isaiah 40:10-11)

Multitudes who sleep in the
dust of the earth will awake,
some to everlasting life, others to
shame and everlasting contempt.
Those who are wise will shine like the
brightness of the heavens,
and those who lead many to
righteousness like the stars
for ever and ever.

(Daniel 12:2-3)

In the movie *Papillon*, the main character was a criminal who was imprisoned for life for crimes against the French state. The film portrayed the dreams he had while in prison. In one dream, he stood before a tribunal for a crime. He pleaded with the judge that he was not guilty for the crime for which he was being tried. The judge replied that he was not being tried for that crime, but for a crime that is the most heinous crime of the human race. Papillon asked what crime it was. He replied, "The crime of a wasted life." Papillon wept, "Guilty, guilty." The judge pronounced the sentence of death.

The greatest possible impact the life of a person without Christ can have on eternity is on the order of a large ship's impact on the ocean. It leaves a wake, which may be very impressive for the moment, but which is gone without a trace within a few moments more. God grant that we invest our lives well by pursuing God's purpose for our lives and by living with a heart for the things He says will endure.

Day 231

WHEN WE ARE AT HOME

Men will see the Son of Man coming in
clouds with great power and glory.
And He will send His angels and gather
His elect from the four winds,
from the ends of the earth to the ends of the heavens.
We must take heed and be watchful,
for we do not know when that time will come.

(Mark 13:26-27, 33)

We will not all sleep, but we will all be changed,
in a moment, in the twinkling of an eye,
at the last trumpet.
For the trumpet will sound, and the dead
will be raised imperishable,
and we shall be changed.
For this perishable must clothe itself
with the imperishable,
and this mortal with immortality.

(1 Corinthians 15:51-53)

Gloriously wasteful, O my Lord, art thou!
Sunset faints after sunset into the night,
Splendorously dying from thy window sill—
For ever. Sad our poverty doth bow
Before the riches of thy making might:
Sweep from thy space thy systems at thy will—
In thee the sun sets every sunset still.

And in the perfect time, O perfect God,
When we are in our home, our natal home,
When joy shall carry every sacred load,
And from its life and peace no heart shall roam,
What if thou make us able to make like thee—
To light with moons, to clothe with greenery,
To hang gold sunsets o'er a rose and purple sea!

Then to his neighbor one may call out, "Come,
Brother, come hither—I would show you a thing";
And lo, a vision of his imagining,
Informed of thought which else had rested dumb,
Before the neighbor's truth-delighted eyes,
In the great ether of existence rise,
And two hearts each to each the closer cling!

George MacDonald,
Diary of an Old Soul

Day 232

SEIZE THE MOMENT

Everything exposed by the light becomes visible,
for it is light that makes everything visible.
For this reason it says, "Awake, you who sleep;
arise from the dead, and Christ will shine on you."

(Ephesians 5:13-14)

Blessed are the dead who die
in the Lord from now on.
They will rest from their labor,
for their works will follow them.

(Revelation 14:13)

❧

In the film, *Dead Poets Society*, Robin Williams plays an English teacher in a private school who makes a dramatic attempt at the near-impossible task of communicating the brevity of life to a group of adolescents. He gathers the students before an old trophy case and invites them to look closely at the faces of an earlier class that graduated some seventy or eighty years before. As the camera slowly pans in to a close-up of the faces in the photograph, we see all the hope and ambition of youth in their eyes and smiles. In the voice-over, Williams tells his students that the people in the photo were just like them, but now they are pushing up daisies. He exhorts them to seize the moment—carpe diem!

The better we understand the brevity of our earthly sojourn, the more we will treasure our opportunities, knowing that what we do in this life echoes in eternity.

Day 233

THE SACRAMENT OF THE PRESENT MOMENT

The kingdom of heaven is like treasure
hidden in a field,
which a man found and hid;
and from his joy, he went and sold all he had
and bought that field.
Again, the kingdom of heaven is like
a merchant looking for fine pearls;
and finding one pearl of great value,
he went away and sold all that he had
and bought it.

(Matthew 13:44-46)

By Your grace, I want to hear the words,
"Well done, good and faithful servant;
you have been faithful with a few things;
I will put you in charge of many things.
Enter into the joy of your Lord."

(Matthew 25:21)

Blaise Pascal prayed in his *Pensées*:

"With perfect consistency of mind, help me to receive all manner of events. For we know not what to ask, and we cannot ask for one event rather than another without presumption. We cannot desire a specific action without presuming to be a judge, and assuming responsibility for what in Your wisdom You may hide from me. O Lord, I know only one thing, and that is that it is good to follow You and wicked to offend You. Beyond this, I do not know what is good for me, whether health or sickness, riches or poverty, or anything else in this world. This knowledge surpasses both the wisdom of men and of angels. It lies hidden in the secrets of Your providence, which I adore, and will not dare to pry open."

We are essentially spiritual beings, and each "today" that is received with gratitude from God's hand contributes to our preparation for our glorious and eternal destiny in His presence. In "the sacrament of the present moment" as Jean-Pierre de Caussade described it, "It is only right that if we are discontented with what God offers us every moment, we should be punished by finding nothing else that will content us" (*Abandonment to Divine Providence*). It is when we learn to love God's will that we can embrace the present moment as a source of spiritual formation.

Day 234

LIVING IN THE POWER OF THE SPIRIT

He who comes from above is above all;
he who is from the earth belongs to the earth,
and speaks as one from the earth.
He who comes from heaven is above all.
He whom God has sent speaks the words of God,
for He gives the Spirit without limit.

(John 3:31, 34)

What the law was powerless to do in that
it was weakened through the flesh,
God did by sending His own Son in the likeness
of sinful flesh, on account of sin;
He condemned sin in the flesh,
in order that the requirement of the law
might be fully met in us,
who do not walk according to the flesh,
but according to the Spirit.

(Romans 8:3-4)

The story has been told of a do-it-yourselfer who went into a hardware store early one morning and asked for a saw. The salesman took a chain saw from the shelf and commented that it was their "newest model, with the latest in technology, guaranteed to cut ten cords of firewood a day." The customer thought that sounded pretty good, so he bought it on the spot.

The next day the customer returned, looking somewhat exhausted. "Something must be wrong with this saw," he moaned. "I worked as hard as I could and only managed to cut three cords of wood. I used to do four with my old-fashioned saw." Looking confused, the salesman said, "Here, let me try it out back on some wood we keep there." They went to the woodpile, the salesman pulled the cord, and as the motor went Vvvrooommm, the customer leaped back and exclaimed, "What's that noise?"

The customer trying to saw wood without the power of the chainsaw to help him is very much like the believer who attempts to live the Christian life without the daily empowerment of the Spirit.

Day 235

WE ARE PILGRIMS AND SOJOURNERS

Here I do not have an enduring city,
but I am seeking the city that is to come.

(Hebrews 13:14)

As an alien and a stranger in the world,
I will abstain from fleshly lusts, which
war against my soul.

(1 Peter 2:11)

Life can be compared to a brief stay in a hotel. In some cases the hotel is a fleabag, and in others, there may be mints on the pillows and flowers on the table. But whatever the hotel's rating, we are still living out of suitcases while we are there. And since we know it is not our home, we don't concern ourselves with changing the decor, even if we dislike the curtains and wallpaper. God never intended room service to replace good home-cooked meals; it is a mistake to confuse hotel life with the glorious dwelling place He is preparing for those who know and love His Son.

Part of our problem is that God's promises seem vague and distant—we have no memories of heaven. But He has given us His word that He will more than make it worth our while. "For here we do not have a lasting city, but we are seeking the city which is to come" (Hebrews 13:14). If we remember that here we are sojourners, strangers, and aliens in exile, our priorities will begin to reflect those of Abraham who "was looking for the city which has foundations, whose architect and builder is God" (Hebrews 11:8-10).

Day 236

THE GOOD CAN BE THE ENEMY OF THE BEST

I do not want to be worried and troubled
about many things;
only one thing is needed.
Like Mary, I want to choose the good part,
which will not be taken away from me.

(Luke 10:41-42)

I will not lay up for myself treasures on earth,
where moth and rust destroy and where
thieves break in and steal.
But I will lay up for myself treasures in heaven,
where moth and rust do not destroy
and where thieves do not break in and steal.
For where my treasure is, there my heart will be also.

(Matthew 6:19-21; Luke 12:34)

Developing an appetite for secondary goods can suppress our appetite for the things that are most important.

One night a mother fixed a special meal for her family: turkey with mashed potatoes and gravy, corn, green beans, cranberry sauce, and apple pie for dessert. It was everyone's favorite meal, especially when it came at a time other than Thanksgiving. The aroma filled the house, and as the children came in from playing, they could hardly wait for dinner to begin. The last child appeared only a few minutes before dinner time and sat through the meal without eating, even though he especially loved those foods. Why? Because he had filled up on peanut butter at a friend's house. In settling for something good, he had lost his appetite for the best.

The same applies to our spiritual appetites. Some people do not have much of an appetite for spiritual truths because they have filled themselves with lesser things.

Day 237

THE HIDDEN BLESSING OF PAIN

The God of all grace, who called me
to His eternal glory in Christ,
after I have suffered a little while,
will Himself perfect, confirm, strengthen,
and establish me.

(1 Peter 5:10)

I will trust in the Lord with all my heart
and lean not on my own understanding;
in all my ways I will acknowledge Him,
and He will make my paths straight.
I will not be wise in my own eyes,
but I will fear the Lord and depart from evil.

(Proverbs 3:5-7)

In *The Problem of Pain*, C. S. Lewis argues that God allows pain in our lives not because He loves us less, but because He loves us more than we would wish:

"Over a sketch made idly to amuse a child, an artist may not take much trouble: he may be content to let it go even though it is not exactly as he meant it to be. But over the great picture of his life—the work which he loves, though in a different fashion, as intensely as a man loves a woman or a mother a child—he will take endless trouble—and would, doubtless, thereby give endless trouble to the picture if it were sentient. One can imagine a sentient picture, after being rubbed and scraped and re-commenced for the tenth time, wishing that it were only a thumb-nail sketch whose making was over in a minute."

As we renew our minds with a growing biblical perspective on the experiences and circumstances of life, we come to see that this life is a time of sowing the seeds of eternity rather than multiplying ephemeral treasures on earth. Such a perspective reduces our anxieties (Matthew 6:25-34), increases our contentment (Philippians 4:11-13; 1 Timothy 6:6-8), and strengthens our trust and hope (Hebrews 6:13-20).

Day 238

JOY MUST BE SHARED

If we have any encouragement from being
united with Christ,
if any comfort from His love,
if any fellowship of the Spirit,
if any affection and compassion,
we should also be like-minded, having the same love,
being one in spirit and one in purpose.

(Philippians 2:1-2)

We should all be of one mind and be sympathetic,
loving as brothers, compassionate, and humble.

(1 Peter 3:8)

———————— ∞ ————————

Karl Barth observed in his *Church Dogmatics* that real joy is not meant to be hoarded by individuals, but shared by people in their relationships with others:

"It must be said that we can have joy, and therefore will it, only as we give it to others .... There may be cases where a man can be really merry in isolation. But these are exceptional and dangerous. . . . It certainly gives us ground to suspect the nature of his joy as real joy if he does not desire — "Rejoice with me" — that at least one or some or many others, as representatives of the rest, should share this joy. . . . We may succeed in willing joy exclusively for ourselves, but we have to realize that in this case, unless a miracle happens (and miracles are difficult to imagine for such a purpose), this joy will not be true, radiant and sincere."

The pleasures of God's many gifts are best appreciated and savored when others participate with us in their enjoyment and wonder. The wellspring of all joy is Jesus Himself, who told His disciples on the night he was betrayed, "These things I have spoken to you so that My joy may be in you, and that your joy may be made full" (John 15:11).

Day 239

IS IT CHANCE
OR A DANCE?

I will remember the works of the Lord; surely,
I will remember Your wonders of long ago.
I will meditate on all Your works
and consider all Your mighty deeds.
Your way, O God, is holy.
What god is so great as our God?
You are the God who works wonders;
You have revealed Your strength among the peoples.
You redeemed Your people with Your power,
the descendants of Jacob and Joseph.

(Psalm 77:11-15)

The Lord has performed mighty deeds with His arm;
He has scattered those who are proud in the
thoughts of their heart.
He has brought down rulers from their thrones and has
lifted up the humble.

(Luke 1:51-52)

☙

Is it chance
or dance moves
the world?

Is the world
blind and dumb
or bloom, festal?
A vain jest,
or holy feast?

Eugene Warren, *"Christographia XIV"*

Our perspective on life, whether temporal or eternal, will determine the set of rules by which we play, the standards and character we pursue, the source of our hope, and the difference between and obedience and disobedience to God's precepts and principles.

Day 240

WE ARE RELATIONAL BEINGS

Jesus did not ask that the Father should take us
out of the world,
but that He protect us from the evil one.
He prayed, "Father, I desire those You have given Me
to be with Me where I am,
that they may behold My glory,
the glory You have given Me
because You loved Me before the
foundation of the world."

(John 17:15, 24)

When we were helpless, at the right time,
Christ died for the ungodly.
For rarely will anyone die for a righteous man,
though perhaps for a good man someone
would even dare to die.
But God demonstrates His own love for us
in that while we were still sinners, Christ died for us.

(Romans 5:6-8)

———————— ∞ ————————

Because the infinite and personal God loves us, He wants us to grow in an intimate relationship with Him; indeed, this is the purpose for which we were created — to know, love, enjoy, and honor the triune Lord of all creation.

Since God is a relational being, the two great commandments of loving Him and expressing this love for Him by loving others are also intensely relational. We were created not only for fellowship and intimacy with God but also with each other. The relational implications of the Christian doctrine of the Trinity are profound. Since we were created in God's image and likeness, we too are relational beings. The better we know God the better we know ourselves. Augustine's prayer for this double knowledge ("May we know Thee, may we know ourselves") reflects the truth that our union with Christ is now overcoming the alienation with God, with ourselves, and with others that occurred at the Fall.

Day 241

THE FOLLY OF OUR CULTURE

Where is the wise man?
Where is the scholar?
Where is the disputer of this age?
Has not God made foolish the wisdom of the world?
But to those whom God has called,
both Jews and Greeks,
Christ is the power of God and the wisdom of God.

(1 Corinthians 1:20, 24)

I know that friendship with the world is
enmity toward God.
Anyone who wants to be a friend of the world
makes himself an enemy of God.

(James 4:4)

— ❧ —

In his book *Love Your God with All Your Mind*, J. P. Moreland makes these perceptive observations on contemporary culture:

"Our society has replaced heroes with celebrities, the quest for a well-informed character with the search for a flat stomach, substance and depth with image and personality. In the political process, the makeup man is more important than the speech writer, and we approach the voting booth, not on the basis of a well-developed philosophy of what the state should be, but with a heart full of images, emotions, and slogans all packed into thirty-second sound bites. The mind-numbing, irrational tripe that fills TV talk shows is digested by millions of bored, lonely Americans hungry for that sort of stuff."

The philosopher Søren Kierkegaard, who died in 1855, speculated about the impact of radio and television long before they were invented. "Suppose someone invented an instrument, a convenient little talking tube which, say, could be heard over the whole land. . . I wonder if the police would not forbid it, fearing that the whole country would become mentally deranged if it were used."

Day 242

LIVING IN THE HOPE OF RESURRECTION

The heavens will vanish like smoke;
the earth will wear out like a garment,
and its inhabitants will die in the same way.
But Your salvation will last forever,
and Your righteousness will never fail.

(Isaiah 51:6)

In the resurrection of the dead,
the body that is sown is perishable,
but it is raised imperishable;
it is sown in dishonor,
but it is raised in glory;
it is sown in weakness,
but it is raised in power;
it is sown a natural body,
but it is raised a spiritual body.
If there is a natural body,
there is also a spiritual body.

(1 Corinthians 15:42-44)

Many years ago, an old farmer brought his family to the big city for the very first time. They had never seen buildings so tall or sights so impressive. The farmer dropped his wife off at a department store and took his son with him to the bank — the tallest of all the buildings. As they walked into the lobby, they saw something else they had never seen before. Two steel doors opened. A rather large and elderly woman walked in, and the big doors closed behind her. The dial over the door swept to the right and then back to the left. The doors opened and a beautiful young woman came walking out.

The farmer was amazed. He turned to his son and said, "You wait right here. I'm going to get your mother and run her through that thing!"

Our bodies gradually age and die, but our living hope is in the Lord Jesus who will receive us to Himself and "transform the body of our humble state into conformity with the body of His glory" (Philippians 3:21).

Day 243

THE QUALITY OF PERSEVERANCE

May our Lord Jesus Christ Himself and God our Father,
who has loved us and has given us eternal consolation
and good hope by grace, comfort our hearts and
strengthen us in every good work and word.

(2 Thessalonians 2:16-17)

Since the day of the Lord will come like a thief,
what kind of person should I be
in holy conduct and godliness
as I look for and hasten the coming of the day of God?
But according to His promise,
I am looking for new heavens and a new earth,
in which righteousness dwells.
Therefore, since I am looking for these things,
I will be diligent to be found by Him in peace,
spotless and blameless.

(2 Peter 3:10-14)

━━━━━━━━━━ ✿ ━━━━━━━━━━

It was perseverance and patience that finally enabled the young Clyde Tombaugh to discover the planet Pluto (which is no longer classified as a planet). Astronomers had already calculated a probable orbit for an object that was causing perturbations in Neptune's orbital movement. Tombaugh took up the search for the suspected planet in March, 1929. He examined scores of telescopic photographs, each showing tens of thousands of star images in pairs under the blink comparator, or dual microscope. It often took three days to scan a single pair of photographs. It was exhausting, eye-straining work, in Tombaugh's own words, "brutal tediousness." The search went on for months. Star by star, Tombaugh examined twenty million images. Finally, on February 18, 1930, as he was blinking a pair of photographs in the constellation Gemini, "I suddenly came upon the image of Pluto!" It was the most dramatic astronomical discovery in nearly one hundred years.

Great achievements do not come cheaply. It requires a combination of vision and hope to persevere and endure the "brutal tediousness" that can discourage and derail the majority of people. The quality of perseverance is a biblical virtue and an evidence of Christlike character (2 Peter 1:5-8).

Day 244

THE QUEST FOR SIGNIFICANCE

Blessed is the one You choose and
bring near to live in Your courts.
We will be satisfied with the goodness
of Your house, of Your holy temple.

(Psalm 65:4)

God will keep me strong to the end,
so that I will be blameless on the day
of our Lord Jesus Christ.
God is faithful, through whom I was
called into fellowship with His Son,
Jesus Christ our Lord.

(1 Corinthians 1:8-9)

━━━━━━━━━━━━━━ ॐ ━━━━━━━━━━━━━━

In Robert Bolt's play, *A Man for All Seasons*, there is a scene in which Richard Rich, an ambitious young man, asks Thomas More for a position in the court of Henry VIII. Instead, More tells Rich that he should become a teacher, not a courtier—"You'd be a good teacher." Rich objects: "And if I were, who would know it?" More's response is illuminating: "Yourself, your friends, your pupils, God; pretty good public that!"

We are called to play in God's great drama, and it is not the size of our role but the audience to whom we play that makes all the difference. If we are ambitious to be impressive before people, we will never attain the true significance we seek. Instead, significance is found in the simple ambition to be pleasing to God and faithful to His calling for our life, whether our part appears to be great or small.

Later in the play, Rich compromises his integrity to attain political prominence, and betrays Thomas More through perjury in order to gain the position of Collector of Revenues for Wales. More is condemned through this treachery, and as Rich leaves the court, More tells him: "You know, Rich, it profits a man nothing to give his soul for the whole world . . . but for Wales?"

Our character will be shaped by the audience to whom we play.

Day 245

A GRASP OF LIFE'S BREVITY

If a man dies, will he live again?
All the days of my hard service
I will wait for my renewal to come.

(Job 14:14)

I make it my ambition to please the Lord,
whether I am at home in the body or away from it.
For we must all appear before
the judgment seat of Christ,
that each one may receive what is due
for the things done while in the body,
whether good or bad.

(2 Corinthians 5:9-10)

Time, like an ever-rolling stream,
Bears all its sons away;
They fly forgotten as a dream
Dies at the op'ning day.

The busy tribes of flesh and blood
With all their cares and fears,
Are carried downward like a flood
And lost in following years.

These verses from Isaac Watts' hymn, *O God, Our Help in Ages Past,* are based on the profound contrast in Psalm 90 between the eternality of God and the brevity of our earthly sojourn. This psalm, written by Moses near the end of his own journey, counsels us to number our days in order to present to God a heart of wisdom (vs. 12). David's meditation in Psalm 39:4-7 develops the same theme:

Lord, make me to know my end,
And what is the extent of my days,
Let me know how transient I am.
Behold, You have made my days as handbreadths,
And my lifetime as nothing in Your sight,
Surely every man at his best is a mere breath.
Surely every man walks about as a phantom;
Surely they make an uproar for nothing;
He amasses riches, and does not know who will gather them.
And now, Lord, for what do I wait?
My hope is in You.

Day 246

FAITHFULNESS IN THE LITTLE THINGS

May those who hope in You not
be ashamed because of me,
O Lord God of hosts;
may those who seek You not
be dishonored because of me,
O God of Israel.

(Psalm 69:6)

I do not want even a hint of immorality,
or any impurity, or greed in my life,
as is proper for a saint.
Nor will I give myself to obscenity, foolish talk,
or coarse joking, which are not fitting,
but rather to giving of thanks.

(Ephesians 5:3-4)

The story has been told of a bank employee who was due for a good promotion. One day at lunch the president of the bank, who happened to be standing behind the clerk in the cafeteria, saw him slip two pats of butter under his slice of bread so they wouldn't be seen by the cashier.

That little act of dishonesty cost him his promotion. Just a few pennies' worth of butter made the difference. The bank president reasoned that if an employee cannot be trusted in little things he cannot be trusted at all.

Our Lord taught that "He who is faithful in a very little thing is faithful also in much; and he who is unrighteous in a very little thing is unrighteous also in much" (Luke 16:10).

Our lives are tapestries that are being woven by the threads of thousands of little decisions. In the spirituality of little things, fidelity in the ordinary affairs of life can build a momentum that carries the freight of the great decisions we make.

Day 247

THE PULLEY OF RESTLESSNESS

Lord, You have said,
"Come to Me, all you who labor and are heavy laden,
and I will give you rest.
Take My yoke upon you and learn from Me,
for I am gentle and humble in heart,
and you will find rest for your souls.
For My yoke is easy, and My burden is light."

(Matthew 11:28-30)

I will trust in the Lord and do good;
I will dwell in the land and feed on His faithfulness.
I will delight myself in the Lord,
and He will give me the desires of my heart.
I will commit my way to the Lord and trust in Him,
and He will bring it to pass.
I will rest in the Lord and wait patiently for Him;
I will not fret because of him who prospers in his way,
with the man who practices evil schemes.

(Psalm 37:3-5, 7)

⠃

The metaphysical poet George Herbert (1593-1633) beautifully expressed how God uses the pulley of restlessness to draw us to Himself, knowing that our hearts can find true rest in Him alone (Matthew 11:28-30).

When God at first made man,
Having a glass of blessings standing by,
Let us (said he) pour on him all we can:
Let the world's riches, which dispursèd lie,
        Contract into a span.

So strength first made a way;
Then beauty flowed, then wisdom, honour, pleasure:
When almost all was out, God made a stay,
Perceiving that alone of all his treasure
        Rest in the bottom lay.

        For if I should (said he)
Bestow this jewel also on my creature,
He would adore my gifts instead of me,
And rest in Nature, not the God of Nature:
        So both should losers be.

        Yet let him keep the rest,
But keep them with repining restlessness:
Let him be rich and weary, that at least,
If goodness lead him not, yet weariness
        May toss him to my breast.

Day 248

CHRISTIANITY IS NOT A PATENT MEDICINE

From Christ's fullness we have all received,
and grace upon grace.
For the law was given through Moses;
grace and truth came through Jesus Christ.

(John 1:16-17)

Your word is truth.

(John 17:17)

Jesus is the way and the truth and the life.
No one comes to the Father except through Him.

(John 14:6)

In matters of religion, spirituality, faith, or God, many people claim that it doesn't matter what you believe, as long as you are sincere and don't hurt others.

If I held such an emaciated view of God, I seriously doubt that I would bother with "religion" at all. On Sunday mornings, I would sleep in at the "Church of the Inner Spring" and hear sermons by Pastor Pillow.

My real interest in Christianity is in whether it can fulfill its promises — and what Christianity promises cannot happen unless Christianity is true. As C. S. Lewis put it:

"Christianity is not a patent medicine. Christianity claims to give an account of facts — to tell you what the real universe is like. Its account of the universe may be true, or it may not, and once the question is really before you, then your natural inquisitiveness must make you want to know the answer. If Christianity is untrue, then no honest man will want to believe it, however helpful it might be: if it is true, every honest man will want to believe it, even if it gives him no help at all."

Day 249

PROCLAIMING TRUTH IN AN AGE OF RELATIVISM

The Scriptures predicted that the Christ should suffer
and rise from the dead on the third day,
and that repentance and forgiveness of sins
should be preached in His name to all nations,
beginning at Jerusalem.

(Luke 24:46-47)

While Jesus was in the world, He was
the light of the world.
For judgment He came into this world,
that those who do not see may see,
and that those who see may become blind.

(John 9:5, 39)

Philosopher Peter Kreeft observed that "today" worships not God but equality. "It fears being right where others are wrong more than it fears being wrong. It worships democracy and resents the fact that God is an absolute monarch. It has changed the meaning of the word honor from being respected because you are superior in some way to being accepted because you are not superior in any way but just like us. The one unanswerable insult, the absolutely worst name you can possibly call a person in today's society, is 'fanatic,' especially 'religious fanatic.' If you confess at a fashionable cocktail party that you are plotting to overthrow the government, or that you are a PLO terrorist or a KGB spy, or that you molest porcupines or bite bats' heads off, you will soon attract a buzzing, fascinated, sympathetic circle of listeners. But if you confess that you believe that Jesus is the Christ, the Son of the living God, you will find yourself suddenly alone, with a distinct chill in the air."

In an age when tolerance is elevated above truth, those who proclaim Christ as Lord of all will not be friends of the world.

Day 250

DEVELOP A SPIRIT OF THANKSGIVING

I will praise You, O Lord my God, with all my heart,
and I will glorify Your name forever.
For great is Your love toward me,
and You have delivered my soul
from the depths of the grave.

(Psalm 86:12-13)

Through Jesus, I will continually offer to God
a sacrifice of praise,
that is, the fruit of lips that give thanks to His name.

(Hebrews 13:15)

⊱⊰

A grandmother is on the beach with her only grandson. As she watches him playing in the surf, a huge wave comes up and carries him away.

In a panic, she desperately pleads to God for his return: "Take me instead—he's my whole life, my only reason for living. Do anything—just save him!"

Miraculously, a second huge wave appears and deposits the child at her feet unharmed. She inspects him briefly, raises her hands toward heaven and loudly proclaims, "He had a hat!"

Nothing ages more quickly than gratitude. As we take the many blessings of our lives for granted, the grace of God degenerates into entitlement. As my friend Ed Dudley used to put it, if we were born on third base, we wake up believing we just hit a triple.

If we are wise, we will not leave gratitude to spontaneous moments, but cultivate a spirit of thanksgiving for all God has done in our past (Deuteronomy 8:2-3, 11-18), contentment with what He is doing in our present (1 Thessalonians 5:16-18), and joyful hope for what He has promised for our future in Christ (1 Peter 1:3-4; 5:10).

Day 251

TRUTH IS NOT DETERMINED BY A MAJORITY VOTE

You revealed Yourself to Moses as
"I AM WHO I AM."

(Exodus 3:14)

You are the Lord, and there is no other;
apart from You there is no God.
From the rising to the setting of the sun,
we know there is none besides You.
You are the Lord, and there is no other.

(Isaiah 45:5-6)

Jesus Christ is the same yesterday, today, and forever.

(Hebrews 13:8)

ളദ

Harry Truman once commented on the importance of polls to leadership with the following insight: "I wonder how far Moses would have gone if he'd taken a poll in Egypt? What would Jesus Christ have preached if he'd taken a poll in Israel? Where would the Reformation have gone if Martin Luther had taken a poll? It isn't the polls or public opinion of the moment that counts. It is right and wrong and leadership—men with fortitude, honesty, and a belief in the right—that makes epochs in the history of the world."

In an age of growing relativism, it is noteworthy that there has been a growing trend in the media and on the internet to solicit public opinion on virtually every topic. There is a vicious circle in which the media influences public opinion, while changing public opinion influences the media.

A bumper sticker reads: "Don't follow me. I'm lost too." "If a blind man guides a blind man, both will fall into a pit" (Matthew 15:14). We do well to remember that neither truth nor virtue can be determined by a majority vote. These are not embedded in subjective and vacillating human opinion, but in the unchanging and revealed Word from the Creator of the cosmos.

Day 252

TREASURING WHAT GOD CALLS IMPORTANT

I do not want to justify myself in the eyes of men;
God knows our hearts,
and what is highly esteemed among men
is detestable in the sight of God.

(Luke 16:15)

I do not want to love praise from men
more than praise from God.

(John 12:43)

W. E. Sangster tells the story of a frightened woman on the *Titanic* who found her place in a lifeboat that was about to be dropped into the raging North Atlantic. She thought suddenly of something she needed in light of death that was breathing down her neck. She asked for permission to go to her stateroom. She was granted just a moment or so, or they would have to leave without her.

She ran across a deck that was already slanted at a dangerous angle. She ran through the gambling room that had money piled in one corner ankle deep. She came to her stateroom and pushed aside her jewelry, reached above her bed and grabbed three small oranges, and found her way back to the lifeboat and got in.

Death had boarded the *Titanic*. One blast of its awful breath had transformed all values. Instantaneously, priceless things had become worthless. Worthless things had become priceless. And in that moment she preferred three small oranges to a crate of diamonds.

Our Lord taught that the things that are highly prized among people are detestable in the sight of God (Luke 16:15). Let us pray for the wisdom of a loose grip on the things that are destined to perish while we diligently lay hold of that which will endure.

Day 253

LEARNING PRUDENCE AND DISCERNMENT

Whoever is wise understands these things;
whoever is discerning knows them.
The ways of the Lord are right;
the righteous will walk in them,
but transgressors will stumble in them.

(Hosea 14:9)

Whatever is true, whatever is noble,
whatever is right, whatever is pure,
whatever is lovely, whatever is of good report—
if anything is excellent or praiseworthy—
I will think about such things.
The things I have learned and received
and heard and seen in those who walk with Christ
I will practice, and the God of peace will be with me.

(Philippians 4:8-9)

— ☙ —

Although the following story is implausible, the twist at the end illustrates the triumph of discernment over pretense:

A defendant was on trial for murder. There was strong evidence indicating guilt, but there was no corpse. In the defense's closing statement the lawyer, knowing that his client would probably be convicted, resorted to a trick. "Ladies and gentlemen of the jury, I have a surprise for you all," the lawyer said as he looked at his watch.

"Within one minute, the person presumed dead in this case will walk into this courtroom ." He looked toward the courtroom door. The jurors, somewhat stunned, all looked on eagerly. A minute passed. Nothing happened. Finally the lawyer said, "Actually, I made up the previous statement. But you all looked on with anticipation. I therefore put to you that you have a reasonable doubt in this case as to whether anyone was killed and insist that you return a verdict of not guilty."

The jury, clearly confused, retired to deliberate. A few minutes later, the jury returned and pronounced a verdict of guilty. "But how?" inquired the lawyer. "You must have had some doubt; I saw all of you stare at the door." The jury foreman replied: "Oh, we did look, but your client didn't."

Wisdom invites us to become discerning and prudent.

Day 254

THE CONFLICT BETWEEN TRUTH AND CULTURE

Whoever is ashamed of Jesus and His words,
the Son of Man will be ashamed of him
when He comes in His glory
and in the glory of the Father and of the holy angels.

(Luke 9:26)

God highly exalted Christ Jesus
and gave Him the name that is above every name,
that at the name of Jesus every knee should bow,
in heaven and on earth and under the earth,
and every tongue should confess that
Jesus Christ is Lord,
to the glory of God the Father.

(Philippians 2:9-11)

Jesus Christ is coming with the clouds,
and every eye will see Him,
even those who pierced Him;
and all the peoples of the earth will mourn
because of Him.
Even so, Amen.

(Revelation 1:7)

———————— ✂ ————————

In his perceptive book, *The Gravedigger File,* Os Guinness discusses three processes that have gripped our culture in recent decades—secularization, privatization, and pluralization. In his words, secularization is the process through which, starting from the center and moving outward, successive sectors of society and culture have been freed from the decisive influence of religious ideas and institutions. Privatization is the process by which modernization produces a cleavage between the public and the private spheres of life and focuses the private sphere as the special arena for the expansion of individual freedom and fulfillment. And pluralization is the process by which the number of options in the private sphere of modern society rapidly multiplies at all levels, especially at the level of worldviews, faiths and ideologies.

In other words, religion is being rendered culturally insignificant, removed from the public square, and reduced in value to one of a myriad of options. Even so, these contemporary cultural forces cannot defeat the power and purposes of the living God who continues to draw people to His Son and to transform them by the power of His indwelling Spirit.

Day 255

THE REALITY OF
THE RISEN CHRIST

I will be strong and courageous, and act.
I will not be afraid or discouraged,
for the Lord God is with me.
He will not fail me or forsake me.

(1 Chronicles 28:20)

I will rejoice in hope, persevere in affliction,
and continue steadfastly in prayer.

(Romans 12:12)

Who is going to harm me if I am eager to do good?
But even if I should suffer for what is right,
I am blessed, and I will not fear
what they fear or be intimidated.

(1 Peter 3:13-14)

WORDS OF SOME FAMOUS CHRISTIAN MARTYRS

In *20 Compelling Evidences That God Exists*, Rob Bowman and I include a chapter on "The Evidence of Those Who Died for Christ." The words of the martyrs (a word that means "witnesses") bear eloquent witness to the reality of the risen Christ in their lives:

"Eighty and six years have I now served Christ, and he has never done me the least wrong: How then can I blaspheme my King and my Savior?"
—Polycarp (70-156), bishop of Smyrna

"You can kill us, but you cannot do us any real harm."
—Justin Martyr (ca. 100-165), Christian apologist

"That which I have taught with my lips, I will now seal with my blood." —Jan Hus (1369-1415), Czech reformer, martyred for his pre-reformation views

"When Christ calls a man, he bids him come and die."
—Dietrich Bonhoeffer (1906-1945), German Lutheran pastor, imprisoned and then executed for his resistance to Hitler

"He is no fool who gives what he cannot keep to gain what he cannot lose." —Jim Elliot (1927-1956), missionary to the Huaorani in Ecuador

Day 256

THERE IS MORE TO LIFE
THAN MEETS THE EYE

The hour is coming and now is,
when true worshipers will worship the Father
in spirit and truth,
for the Father is seeking such to worship Him.
God is spirit, and those who worship Him
must worship in spirit and truth.

(John 4:23-24)

He who believes in You, as the Scripture has said,
rivers of living water will flow from within him,
because Your Spirit indwells him.

(John 7:38-39)

In the popular science-fiction movie *The Matrix*, Keanu Reeves plays an ordinary man who is not ordinary at all. But then, everything that seems ordinary turns out not to be real. Reeves' character, called Neo — a tip-off that he is the first of a new kind of man — learns that his whole world is actually a "virtual reality" illusion called "the Matrix" that was created by alien machines that have taken over the Earth. He and the rest of humanity have been living a lie. At first, the truth is very hard to accept, and Neo finds it difficult to make the transition from the "virtual" world to the "real" world.

The Matrix is a thought-provoking film on many levels. There is, however, one way to ruin it entirely, and that is to take it too seriously. Like much science fiction, The Matrix is best understood as a parable. At its heart, the film provokes the viewer to consider the possibility that reality is larger than the familiar material world that we experience through our five senses. There is more to life than meets the eye, but this does not mean that all is illusion.

Day 257

LIBERTY IS A GIFT OF GOD

The Lord has said, "If My people who
are called by My name
will humble themselves and pray and seek My face
and turn from their wicked ways,
then I will hear from heaven
and will forgive their sin and heal their land."

(2 Chronicles 7:14)

I will submit myself to the governing authorities.
For there is no authority except from God,
and the authorities that exist have been
established by God.
Consequently, he who resists authority
has opposed the ordinance of God,
and those who do so
will bring judgment on themselves.

(Romans 13:1-2)

—————————————— ☙ ——————————————

As the following sample quotes make clear, contemporary political revisionism has distanced us from the vision of early American leaders:

"We have staked the whole future of American civilization, not upon the power of government, far from it. We have staked the future of all of our political institutions upon the capacity of mankind of self-government; upon the capacity of each and all of us to govern ourselves, to control ourselves, to sustain ourselves according to the Ten Commandments of God." — James Madison

"Can the liberties of a nation be thought secure when we have removed their only firm basis, a conviction in the minds of the people that these liberties are the gift of God?" — Thomas Jefferson

"If we abide by the principles taught in the Bible, our country will go on prospering and to prosper; but if we and our posterity neglect its instructions and authority, no man can tell how sudden a catastrophe may overwhelm us and bury all our glory in profound obscurity." — Daniel Webster

"I believe the Bible is the best gift God has ever given to man. All the good from the Saviour of the world is communicated to us through this book." — Abraham Lincoln

Day 258

THE VALUE OF INTEGRITY

I will not accept a bribe,
for a bribe blinds those who see
and perverts the words of the righteous.

(Exodus 23:8)

I will not say when I am tempted,
"I am being tempted by God;"
for God cannot be tempted by evil,
nor does He tempt anyone.
But each one is tempted when he is drawn away
and enticed by his own lust.
Then, after lust has conceived, it gives birth to sin;
and sin, when it is full-grown, gives birth to death.

(James 1:13-15)

———————— ೮೦ ————————

After his Sunday messages, the pastor of a church in London got on the trolley Monday morning to go back to his study downtown. He paid his fare, and the trolley driver gave him too much change.

The pastor sat down and fumbled the change and looked it over, then counted it several times. You know the rationalization, "It's wonderful how God provides." He realized he was tight that week and this was just about what he would need to break even, or at least enough for his lunch. He wrestled with himself all the way down that old trolley trail that led to his office. And finally he came to the stop and he got up, couldn't live with himself, walked up to the trolley driver, and said, "Here, you gave me too much change. You made a mistake."

The driver said, "No, it was no mistake. You see, I was in your church last night when you spoke on honesty, and I thought I would put you to the test."

Our character is evident in what we are and do when we think no one is looking. With people of integrity, there is a growing congruity between what they are and do on the inside and what they are and do on the outside.

Day 259

STANDING FIRM
IN THE TRUTH

All Scripture is God-breathed and is useful
for teaching, for reproof, for correction,
for training in righteousness,
that the man of God may be thoroughly equipped
for every good work.

(2 Timothy 3:16-17)

The law of the Lord is perfect, restoring the soul.
The testimony of the Lord is sure,
making wise the simple.
The precepts of the Lord are right, rejoicing the heart.
The commandment of the Lord is pure,
enlightening the eyes.
The fear of the Lord is clean, enduring forever.
The judgments of the Lord are true
and altogether righteous.
They are more desirable than gold, than much pure gold;
they are sweeter than honey, than honey from the comb.
Moreover, by them is Your servant warned;
in keeping them there is great reward.

(Psalm 19:7-11)

━━━━━━━━━━━━━━━━ ಐ ━━━━━━━━━━━━━━━━

H. Richard Niehbur once described late nineteenth century liberalism in these remarkably succinct words: "A God without wrath brought men without sin into a kingdom without judgment through the ministrations of a Jesus without a cross." In recent decades, this distorted and emaciated gospel has also been seeping into the thinking and practice of popular Christendom. Terms like "wrath," "sin," "judgment," and "cross" do not play well in a culture that has come to regard tolerance as more virtuous than truth. Through careful use of "text management," we selectively focus on biblical images we want to hear and avoid the things in Scripture that seem harsh to our modern ears.

Notice how both John the Baptist and our Lord in His early Galilean ministry both proclaimed the same disturbing message: "Repent, for the kingdom of heaven is at hand" (Matthew 3:2; 4:17). How well do you think these words would go over in the average church today? We would be wise to consider how tightly we have been gripped by the cultural agendas of our times and renew our minds by aligning our thinking with the whole counsel of Scripture.

Day 260

TREATING OTHERS WITH KINDNESS

"You shall love the Lord your God
with all your heart and with all your soul
and with all your mind."
This is the first and great commandment.
And the second is like it:
"You shall love your neighbor as yourself."
All the Law and the Prophets hang on
these two commandments.

(Matthew 22:37-40)

I will owe nothing to anyone except to love them,
for he who loves his neighbor has fulfilled the law.
For the commandments,
"You shall not commit adultery,"
"You shall not murder," "You shall not steal,"
"You shall not covet," and if there is any
other commandment,
it is summed up in this saying:
"You shall love your neighbor as yourself."
Love does no harm to a neighbor;
therefore love is the fulfillment of the law.

(Romans 13:8-10)

———————— ℔ ————————

In the days when an ice cream sundae cost much less, a ten-year-old boy entered a hotel coffee shop and sat at a table. A waitress put a glass of water in front of him. "How much for an ice cream sundae?"

"Fifty cents," replied the waitress.

The little boy pulled his hand out of his pocket and studied a number of coins in it. "How much is a dish of plain ice cream?" he inquired.

Some people were now waiting for a table and the waitress was a bit impatient. "Thirty-five cents," she said brusquely.

The little boy again counted the coins. "I'll have the plain ice cream," he said.

The waitress brought the ice cream, put the bill on the table, and walked away. The boy finished the ice cream, paid the cashier, and departed. When the waitress came back, she picked up the empty plate and then swallowed hard at what she saw. There, placed neatly beside the empty dish, were two nickels and five pennies—her tip.

Every day we will encounter little annoyances that are opportunities in disguise. As Thomas Dubay put it in *The Evidential Power of Beauty*, "if people who annoy me are also God's beloved, they must be mine as well: we are to love as he loves us (Jn 13:34)."

ॐ

Day 261

THE PROMISE OF REWARD

There is no one who has left house or brothers
or sisters or mother or father or children or fields
for Your sake and the gospel's,
who will not receive a hundred times
as much in this present age—
houses, brothers, sisters, mothers,
children and fields, along with persecutions—
and in the age to come, eternal life.

(Mark 10:29-30)

Those who are rich in this present world
should not be arrogant or set their hope on the
uncertainty of riches
but on God, who richly provides us with
everything for our enjoyment.
They should do good, be rich in good works,
and be generous and willing to share.
In this way they will lay up treasure for themselves
as a firm foundation for the future,
so that they may lay hold of true life.

(1 Timothy 6:17-19)

332

In his sermon on *The Weight of Glory*, C. S. Lewis distinguishes two kinds of reward:

"We must not be troubled by unbelievers when they say that this promise of reward makes the Christian life a mercenary affair. There are different kinds of reward. There is the reward which has no natural connection with the things you do to earn it, and is quite foreign to the desires that ought to accompany those things. Money is not the natural reward of love; that is why we call a man a mercenary if he married a woman for the sake of her money. But marriage is the proper reward for a real lover, and he is not mercenary for desiring it. . . . The proper rewards are not simply tacked on to the activity for which they are given, but are the activity itself in consummation."

Rewards in the kingdom of heaven are based on our faithfulness to the opportunities we have been given during our earthly lives. These rewards are the consummation of the pursuit of God.

Day 262

EXTRA GRACE REQUIRED

If I speak in the tongues of men and of angels,
but have not love, I am only a resounding
gong or a clanging cymbal.
And if I have the gift of prophecy and understand all
mysteries and all knowledge,
and if I have all faith so as to remove mountains,
but have not love, I am nothing.
And if I give all my possessions to the poor,
and if I deliver my body to be burned,
but have not love, it profits me nothing.

(1 Corinthians 13:1-3)

I will be an imitator of God as a beloved child,
and I will walk in love, just as Christ loved me
and gave Himself up for me as a fragrant
offering and sacrifice to God.

(Ephesians 5:1-2)

၆

Harpo [Arthur] Marx (1893-1964) was the member of the famous Marx Brothers comedy team who pretended to be dumb. He was a skilled harpist.

During a visit to New York, Harpo was plagued by representatives of charities wanting him to appear at benefits. One persistent lady telephoned him no fewer than twelve times in forty-eight hours. Harpo eventually agreed to appear for her charity. To ensure that he would not escape her at the last minute, she called to escort him personally to the benefit. As they were leaving his hotel suite, the telephone began ringing. "Don't you want to go back and answer it? the lady asked. "Why bother?" responded Harpo with a weary sigh. "It's undoubtedly you again."

All of us have experienced the draining effects of people who sometimes play the role of an "EGR" in our lives— "Extra Grace Required." Before we respond with avoidance and criticism, we would do well remember that we may play a similar role with others, and we certainly do before God.

Kenneth Boa

Kenneth Boa is engaged in a ministry of relational evangelism and discipleship, teaching, writing and speaking. He holds a B.S. from Case Institute of Technology, a Th.M. from Dallas Theological Seminary, a Ph.D. from New York University, and a D.Phil. from the University of Oxford in England.

Dr. Boa is the President of Reflections Ministries, an organization that seeks to encourage, teach, and equip people to know Christ, follow Him, become progressively conformed to His image, and reproduce His life in others. He is also President of Trinity House Publishers, a publishing company that is dedicated to the creation of tools that will help people manifest eternal values in a temporal arena by drawing them to intimacy with God and a better understanding of the culture in which they live.

Recent publications by Dr. Boa include *Conformed to His Image, 20 Compelling Evidences that God Exists, Face to Face, Augustine to Freud, Faith Has its Reasons,* and *God, I Don't Understand.* He is a contributing editor to *The Open Bible* and *The Leadership Bible,* and the consulting editor of the *Zondervan NASB Study Bible.*

Kenneth Boa also writes a free monthly teaching letter called *Reflections.* If you would like to be on the mailing list, visit KenBoa.org or call 800-DRAW NEAR (800-372-9632).